ARCHITECTURE AND MEDIA

CONTENTS

Editor's Note 4

Dream House

Dream Home: Architecture and Mass Media 6
Su Wen

Water Tank House 8
Liu Yichun + Liu Kenan | Atelier Deshaus + Atelier XUK

Home for a Veteran 18
Zhang Ming + Zhang Zi | Original Design Studio / TJAD

Aranya Effect

The Instagram Archive of Aranya Holiday Resort: Image Creation Beyond the Camera Lens 24
Wang Xuerui

Seashore Library 28
Dong Gong | Vector Architects

Seashore Chapel 38
Dong Gong | Vector Architects

Aranya Art Center 46
Lyndon Neri + Rossana Hu | Neri&Hu Design and Research Office

UCCA Dune Art Museum 56
Li Hu + Huang Wenjing | OPEN Architecture

2 Architecture China

Architects' Strategies

Game of Capitals: 66
The Production of Influential
Online Architecture
Zhao Xiaoxin

Recent Projects

Tiantai No. 2 Primary School 74
Ruan Hao + Zhan Yuan | LYCS Architecture

The Chuan Malt Whisky Distillery 102
Lyndon Neri + Rossana Hu | Neri&Hu Design and Research Office

Service Station Under Wuning Road Bridge 124
Zhou Wei & Zhang Bin | Atelier Z+

Tai'an Dongximen Village Revitalization 80
Meng Fanhao + Zhu Peidong | line+ studio

798CUBE Art Museum 110
Zhu Pei | Studio Zhu Pei

Hunan Street Integrated Service Station 132
Yuan Ye + Zhang Ziyue | Steam Architecture

News 142

Editor's note

Architecture as Social Media Influencer: A Makeshift Strategy for Rapidly Evolving Consumer Cities

Li Xiangning
Editor in Chief, Architecture China
Professor, College of Architecture and Urban Planning, Tongji University

From the Aranya Seashore Library, often called the "Loneliest Library," to Changsha's Wenheyou, famous for its long lines of eager visitors, the relationship between architecture and media has never been closer than it is today. Many buildings are gaining renewed attention thanks to social media, transforming architecture into a powerful influencer and this shift is challenging traditional perspectives in the architecture industry.

The concept of architecture as an influencer is not new. It happened before in the 1990s, in the Spanish city of Bilbao. After the decline of its steel and shipbuilding industries, the city found new life through setting up a new museum. In 1997, the world-renowned Guggenheim Museum opened its doors, revitalizing the area and generating hundreds of millions of dollars in economic returns. The media referred to this phenomenon as the "Bilbao effect," and the Guggenheim Museum became one of the first prominent cases of architecture serving as an influencer through media.

This phenomenon is sometimes unintentional on the part of the architects. In 2008, the proposal for the new CCTV Headquarters in Beijing was pushed "out of the loop" because it resembled a pair of "big trousers." The building's unique design and high cost raised questions, but it also presented a challenge to the traditional image of high-rise buildings. While it is difficult to measure the building's success, it did garner significant global publicity for CCTV.

Since the advent of the modern architectural movement, architecture has been closely linked with mass media. Beatrice Colomina, an American architectural scholar, has examined the works of modernist masters such as Le Corbusier and Adolf Loos from this perspective. In today's social media era, the term "celebrity architecture" refers to the impact that a building has on social media, rather than imply any assessment on its architectural value.

Contemporary Chinese architecture first gained widespread public attention in 2014 with the broadcast of *Dream Home*, a TV program that showcased the innovative thinking behind the designs of selected architects, and the stories that inspired them, in such a way that was accessible to the general audience. Unlike in the past, when the media often focused solely on the finished structures, *Dream Home* combined architecture with storytelling. It highlighted the daily lives of the people connected to the buildings, emphasizing that storytelling has become an essential aspect of contemporary architecture.

Also, in 2014, the new media architecture platform Yi Tiao featured an article titled "The Loneliest Library," which highlighted architect Dong Gong's work as one of the most significant media landmarks in contemporary China. With the rise of the WeChat era, the article quickly gained over 100,000 readers.

These two events were a good foretelling of the close relationship between contemporary Chinese architecture and media, particularly social media, in the coming decade. Whether it is actively intended or simply accepted, taking photos of architectural works and sharing them on social networks has become woven as an essential layer of existence today.

In the past, people experienced and interacted with physical spaces in person, but today, taking pictures has become a significant way to engage with architecture. To some extent, the influence of a building in contemporary society—its effect on public space—often pales in comparison to its presence on social media. If we consider architecture as both a tangible entity and a dynamic alternative in the digital realm, its symbolic significance may surpass its physical value. The number of likes a building receives on social media is increasingly becoming a measure of its success. The traditional idea of "form follows function" is being challenged by the concept of "form follows media."

The phenomenon of architecture acting as a social media influencer has sparked our imagination about contemporary cities. Recent discussions on urban development in China have highlighted a persistent concern: the absence of local culture. On one hand, there is a growing discourse on how Chinese cities can embody a sense of "Chinese-ness" while also exploring the unique characteristics of each city. On the other hand, amidst the inevitable processes of urban gentrification and rapid technological advancement, it remains challenging for fast-developing cities to genuinely reflect on their identities and ask meaningful questions about themselves.

How then should architects navigate architecture as influencers or "form follows media"? In the early 20th century, classical orders were often seen as the standard for authentic architecture. However, the renowned architect Le Corbusier introduced the "Five Points of the New Architecture" during the same period. Initially regarded as a passing trend, these Five Points have since become one of the most significant theories in the field of architecture. Similarly, studying Corbusier today involves not just his architectural work but also examining how he responded to new ideas and developed a unique language.

This issue of *Architecture China* aims to showcase the diverse perspectives and critical reflections of contemporary Chinese architects in relation to social media and its influence on architecture. In summarizing the fifth generation of Chinese architects, I have proposed the concept of "makeshift architecture." This group of young architects is well-versed in the trends and characteristics of Western architecture, while also having a deep understanding of China's current circumstances and limitations. As a result, they have developed a series of "expedient" architectural strategies. In today's age of social media and increasing urban mobility, architecture faces greater uncertainty. The balance between "looking back" at traditional methods and "looking forward" toward future possibilities may necessitate a makeshift approach to media engagement. This requires a thoughtful balance between the ultimate goals of architecture and the realities of the present, allowing architects to navigate the rapid changes of our time effectively.

Dream Home: Architecture and Mass Media

Su Wen
PhD candidate
College of Architecture and Planning, Tongji University

Since it aired in 2014, the Shanghai TV variety show *Dream Home* has been running successfully for seven seasons, garnering wide praise for its consistent high quality and being among the top tier of other similar shows. In each episode, a common living space with challenging characteristics is chosen and transformed into a new and improved residential space by inviting architects and designers to review existing interior conflicts and executing renovations to fit. Not only has the show become a successful representative of its genre, but it has also brought many outstanding architects to public attention, such as Aoyama Shuhei, Zhang Ming, and Liu Yichun.

The biggest attraction of such a program is the "before" and "after" looks in the home transformation. The dramatic renovation of a complex living environment full of obstacles into an ideal living space creates surprise and excitement among the viewers while simultaneously highlighting the architects' skill in remodeling diverse spaces. The advanced technologies and ingenious ideas they employ during the renovation process are the key factors for the successful transformation of the houses. For example, in the second episode of the first season, architect He Yongming came up with the creative idea of installing mirrors on top of a tall building in order to reflect light down into the apartments inside a very narrow alleyway. In the first episode of the second season, architect Yu Ting fitted sixteen windows in a water tower used as a residential apartment featuring a complex interior spatial distribution in order to simultaneously solve lighting and ventilation issues. In the first episode of the fifth season, architect Zhang Ming introduced a new functional framework into a dilapidated traditional ancestral home of about 200 square meters by using new industrially produced slide-out modules and yet still preserved the structure's original layout.

As a variety show aimed at the general public, *Dream Home* not only offers new and exciting experiences brought on by technical transformations, but also delicately integrates emotional narratives into the production of the show. In fact, the home transformation in each episode is always accompanied by a heart-wrenching story of hardship or misfortune. By installing the mirrors He Yongming solved the lighting problem in the narrow alleyway in order to fulfill the wish of a father who wanted his daughter to see the sunlight as soon as she wakes up; Yu Ting remodeled the interior of the water tower to meet the necessities of a family who had been living in a humble, not-designed-for-residence space for many years; Zhang Ming's transformation of the traditional house not only showcased the renovation of an ancestral home to preserve its architectural culture, but it was also a tribute to a veteran who devoted his life to serving his country. By reaching out to ordinary and even marginalized families living in modest conditions, this humanistic care for the other has been a part of the show from the very beginning. The show's obvious concern for the living conditions of people with chronic illnesses and disabilities further enhances the program's intellectual and emotional depth and breadth. The stories featured on the program create awareness of and compassion toward the families' plights and sometimes also evoke viewers' empathy as they themselves may have been or be in a similar circumstance and can relate to the struggles of the families. Additionally, the architects' attention to the intricacies of people's lives, their spatial designs for those with special needs, and their efforts to balance neighborly relations during the renovation process add a sense of humanity.

The spatial renovation process and the development of the families' stories are intertwined, together forming the core narrative of *Dream Home*. This dual narrative is embedded in a clear logic: the transformation of a space signifies an improvement to the quality of life. The architects in the program intervene in a material living space, yet the final result is not only the tangible renewal and optimization of the space itself, but also the solution to the occupants' troubles in life. At a certain level, the extreme spatial conditions people live in are a reflection of the contradictions and dilemmas in their lives, while the confined rooms and irrational spatial layouts and usages also amplify the residents' existing hardships and reinforce their suffering. Conversely, changes to their living space can positively impact the occupants' lives, meaning that their misfortunes feel less pronounced or overwhelming through the improvement of their living space. According to this logic, the architect as the main person in charge of the project takes on the responsibility to change the fate of the residents by transforming their living space. This was why, in one episode, the architects' withdrawal from an unfinished project caused widespread indignation among viewers.

In *Dream Home*, the "living space" becomes an intermediary. The intervention by the architects is not so much a modification of the space itself, but rather an overall organization and revision of the residential activities within it. Throughout the show, the architects need to negotiate and communicate constantly with the homeowners, consult with professionals about specific renovation methods, coordinate patiently and tactfully with the neighbors, and even live with the homeowners for a period of time in order to understand the requirements and elements of their daily lives that may affect the space and how they use it. The final result of the information collected from these stages in the process is reflected in the material space, ranging from modified handles, special cabinet doors, railings, or auxiliary facilities. Behind the new spatial order shines the brilliance of the architect's rational thinking and determination to improve the situation. The sense of wonder created by the home transformations illuminates this brilliance on the TV screen, elevating the architect from a skilled renovator into a hero; he/she saves people from the misfortunes of their daily hardships while simultaneously sculpting his/her on-screen identity.

If we consider only image of the architects , then for sure the narrative of *Dream Home* has fulfilled its mission, for many of the architects who participated in the show have become stars themselves, popular with viewers and sought after by investors. This is not only due to their superb technical abilities, but also their demonstrated strong rationality and persuasiveness. The show presents the architects' subjectivity, their abilities, and values with great vigor, even enabling their public image to positively influence their businesses.

With *Dream Home* ultimately still being a TV program and hence requiring a tone of sensationalism, the producers consciously choose the most provocative homes requiring the most dramatic renovation scenarios. The "before-and-after" transformations of the houses; the ingenious ideas of the architects— these elements can be arranged to produce the show's desired effect. But the transformed living spaces themselves will have to respond to much longer and more specific usage scenarios after the filming of the show ends. This presents another opportunity for a dramatic conflict between renovation ideals and reality. In the show's third season, the producers included return visits to earlier featured homes examine the present living conditions of the occupants. It turned out that the transformed buildings were not quite used as the architects and the show's crew had intended. The elevator access designed for an elderly woman suffering from reduced mobility was forcibly demolished as it took up part of the public space and was cluttered with debris from the neighbors. The studio for a designer was left unused due to its limited access and reverted back to a dumping ground for rubble. The height-adjustable table for a translation teacher suffering from ankylosing spondylitis fulfilled its intended function, but often broke down due to its frequent use and therefore required constant maintenance. The skylight installed for a big-boned woman was blocked because she needed a space to dry her clothes. Such problems were revealed during these return visits. It was also discovered that the house in the water tower designed by Yu Ting had been emptied and demolished due to new land use requirements; the owner had lived in the transformed house for less than a year, thus rendering the entire renovation fundamentally futile.

Even though the designers participating in the show used all of their wisdom and resources in planning out the projects, faced with the reality of everyday life their ideas were sometimes more or less invalidated. Although some netizens expressed regret and even indignation at some of the owners' "destruction" of the intended designs, we cannot help but recognize the underlying issue here: when considered from a point of common sense, we have to acknowledge that even if we maximize the regular operation of the spatial order, the intention of these complex spatial designs to overcome extreme spatial constraints will inevitably create a lot of dead corners, accumulate dust, and even age and degrade over time. Moreover, the inertia and fatigue of human beings will render many functional facilities that require an additional operational step useless in the long run. Furthermore, changes in the number of family members and living habits will result in the disruption of the original layout of many of the spaces. In short, we cannot escape the fact that the intended design order gradually loses its grip on daily life and surrenders to time and the occupants' everyday routines.

From this standpoint the architects are caught in a dilemma: they must complete the project to the greatest extent possible within extreme time constraints in front of the camera, and also bring about order and rationality by regaining control and correcting and arranging all of the spatial resources. But this also implies the maximal replacement of the natural entropy generated by the previous mode of living in the space, which is bound to backfire in the long and repetitive cycle of everyday life. As we can see, the ghost of Jane Jacobs's critique of Le Corbusier's elitist rationality still manifests itself today in more concrete and subtle contexts. Ultimately, this is a more profound issue, which involves the struggle and confrontation between the forces of reason and the forces of nature. We can't elevate a rational order to the status of a god, commanding and criticizing people's natural life from above, for it is still us and we ourselves who are living and creating this life. We can treat the houses like a battlefield, similar to Ursula from the novel *One Hundred Years of Solitude* by Gabriel García Márquez, who sprays insecticide on the moths that gnaw at the walls, going by the personal mandate "even the smallest and most useless corner of the house must not fall prey to the bugs." But whether we are strong enough to fight off the ants that eventually eat the last member of Ursula's family is a question that deserves to be reflected upon not only by the architects, but also by every single member of the show's audience. Moreover, by raising this question, *Dream Home* acts not only as a platform for the promotion of architects, but also as a potential medium for everyone to think about architecture and life.

However, there have been also some objectively positive examples shown during the return visits, which illustrate how many of the residents actually make practical use of and extend the function of the spaces that have been remodeled. The fifth season featured an interesting example of this: the apartment designed by architect Takafumi Homma for a young man with the degenerative disease ataxia had remained essentially the same as it was after the renovation, without much change to the space caused by his everyday life. In contrast, the ailing young man continued to rely on the facilities installed during the renovation for his ongoing rehabilitation, constantly struggling with his weakening body. The natural law of his body's decline and the passage of time have not resulted in any substantial alterations to the space or his life. Perhaps the reason for this finds itself in his continuous coexistence and struggle with the forces of nature at play in his daily life. Put another way, there are still people living within the renovated spaces, following the designer's rationale and intended orders, and finding a tense balance in their lives. In this sense, the architect's concept can be more than a guideline, but rather a support system and a companion, giving strength to the people who, though living humbly, are trying to live a long and comfortable life.

Water Tank House

Liu Yichun + Liu Kenan | Atelier Deshaus + Atelier XUK

Location: Shanghai, China
Architect: Atelier Deshaus + Atelier XUK
Principal architect: Liu Yichun (Atelier Deshaus), Liu Kenan (Atelier XUK)
Design team: Wang Longhai, Li Ang, Shen Wen, Zhou Peiyi, Liu Ran, Chang Hongliang, Ke Mingen, Wang Zhili
Gross floor area: 68 square meters
Design period: July 2015
Completion: September 2015
Photography: Atelier XUK
Episode: *Dream House*, Season 2, Episode 11

The Water Tank House was once a disused free-standing water tower in a typical *lilong* neighborhood in Shanghai. During the urbanization process, it was gradually occupied as a residential space. When the water tower was first built, neither its shape, scale nor even the qualities of the space were considered at all for the possibility that it might one day be used as accommodation. When it lost its function as a water tower, the structure was occupied as a space for dwelling. The congested living condition inside the water tower and the complexity associated with its structure is further exacerbated by its changing occupants over the last 50 years.

Aerial view

Water Tank House in context

Night view

The Water Tank House is only one of the seven small-scale homes in the water tower. Its lowest part is only 2 meters high and the minimum clear height is only 1.65 meters. The scale experience in the design is strictly based on the actual height of the inhabitants to determine the necessary interior clearances and access to the upper and lower floors. The focus of the design is on expanding the perception of the interior space. The size of a home may not be expandable, but by using design manipulations the perception of the interior space can be made larger. For example, the use of windows and their out-projecting elements draw the view in while simultaneously proffering certain activities of inside to the outside, thus extending the perception of the interior space. The water tank space at the top is an important part of expanding the interior living space. In conjunction with the small staircase leading to the roof, the architects designed two small patios that act as two inner courtyards. The interior of the house is lit and ventilated through these two patios. Although the exterior remains the same as the original water tank, the interior has been enlivened.

The renovation of the outdoor staircase was the result of a conversation with a neighbor. The renovated staircase is intended to provide more comfortable access for the elderly residents as well as a pleasant outdoor space for the seven families inhabiting the water tower. By creating a public space in the neighborhood, the project has thus become a case for community micro-regeneration.

Looking out from the kitchen toward the staircase

Renovation process

Storage space integrated with the staircase

Staircase and structure detail

Bedroom

Children's space

Staircase

Bedroom

Yard

View from bedroom toward the yard

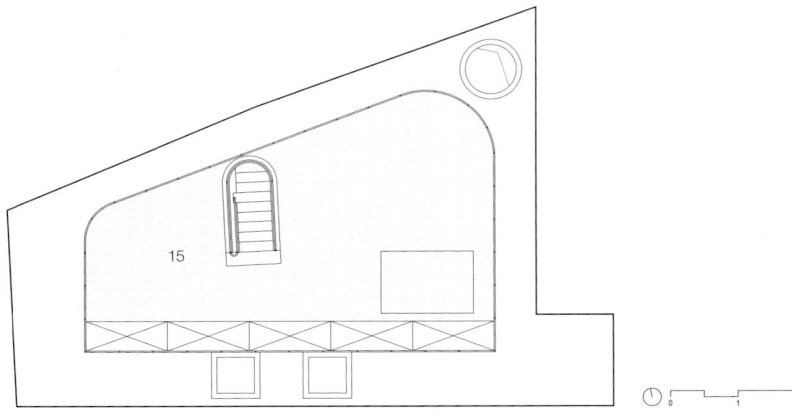

Rooftop floor plan

1. Public corridor
2. Entrance
3. Dining room
4. Kitchen
5. Balcony
6. Washroom 1
7. Grandparents' room
8. Kid's bed/grandpa's desk
9. Exterior space
10. Parents' room
11. Living room/daughter's room
12. Washroom 2
13. Yard 1
14. Yard 2
15. Rooftop

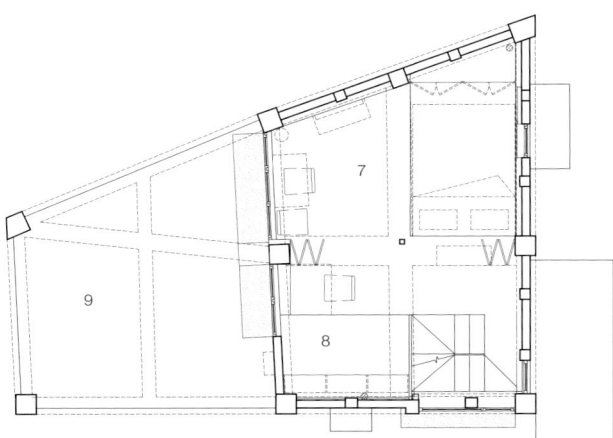

Third-floor plan

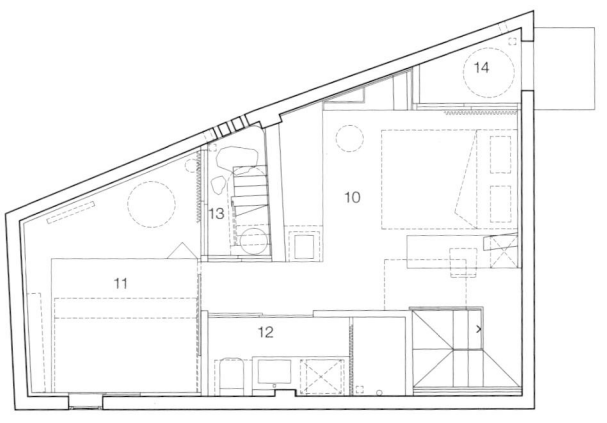

Fourth-floor plan

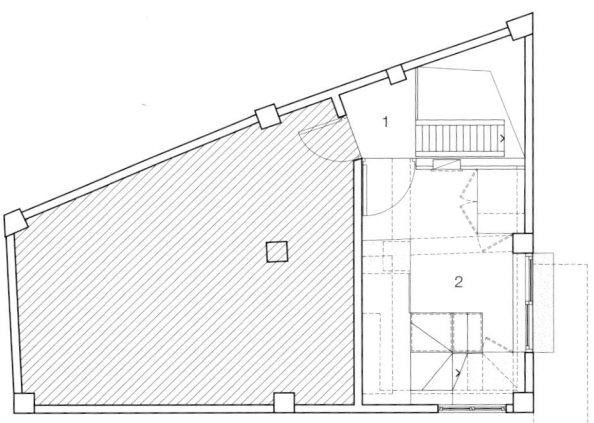

First-floor plan

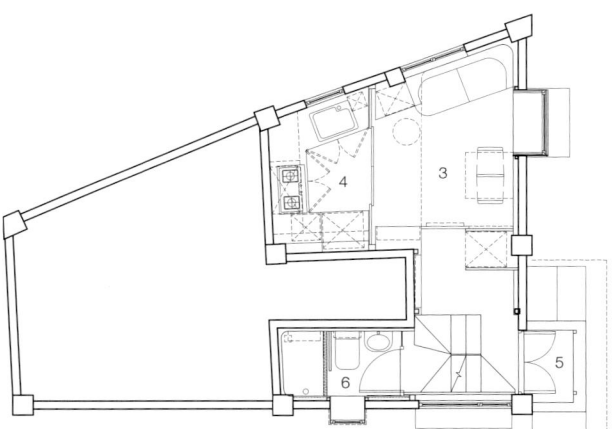

Second-floor plan

Renovated section in watercolor by Ke Mingen

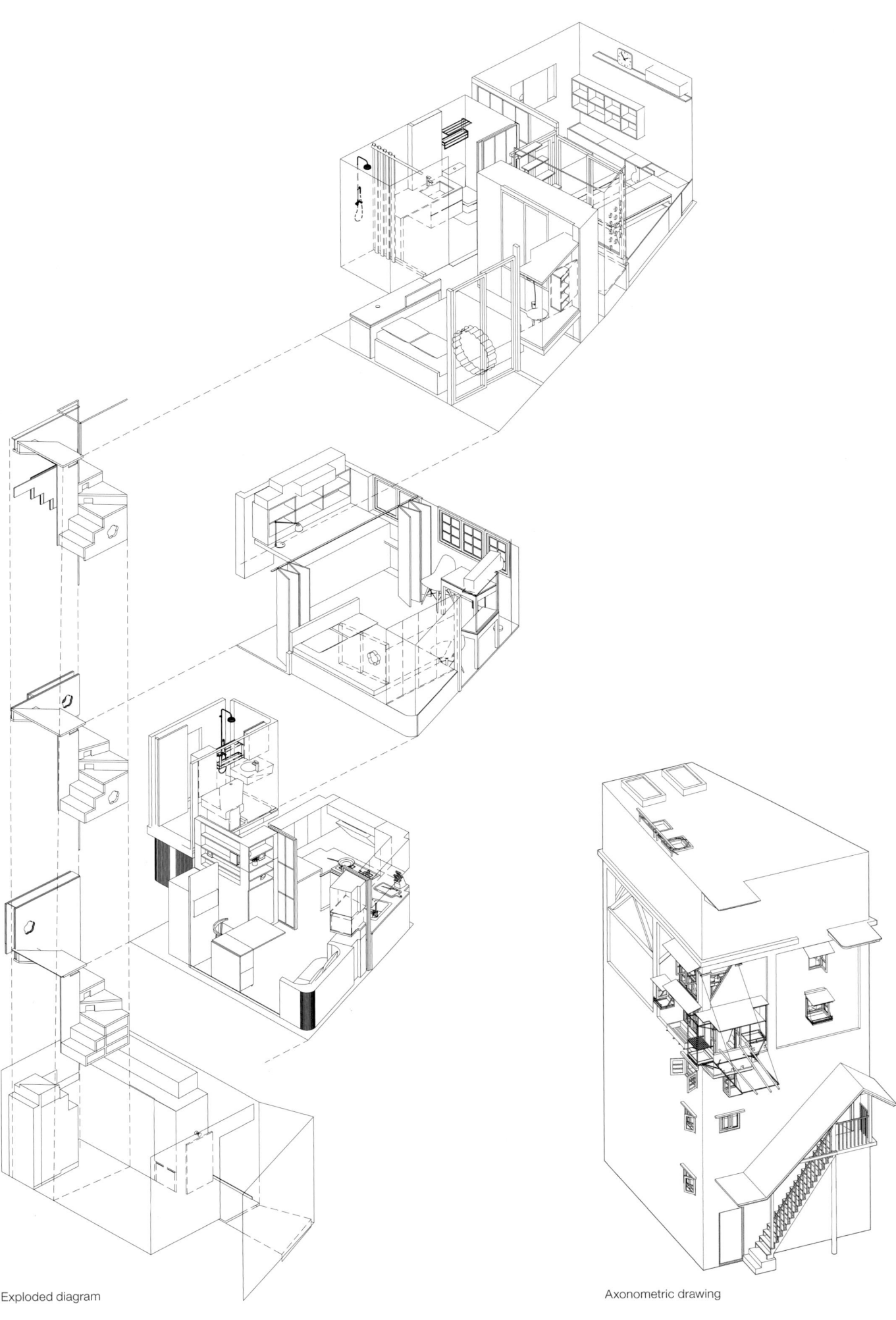

Exploded diagram

Axonometric drawing

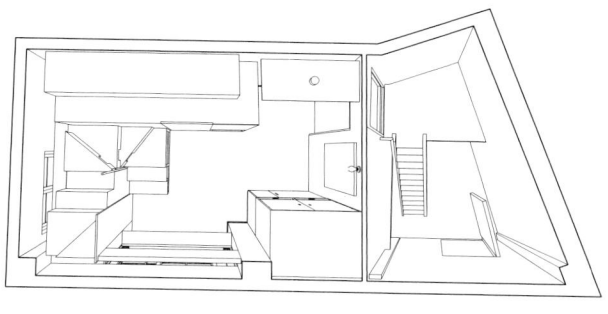
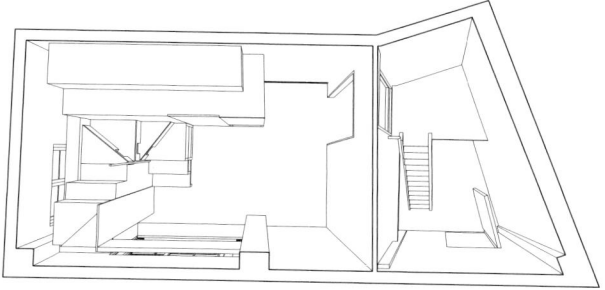
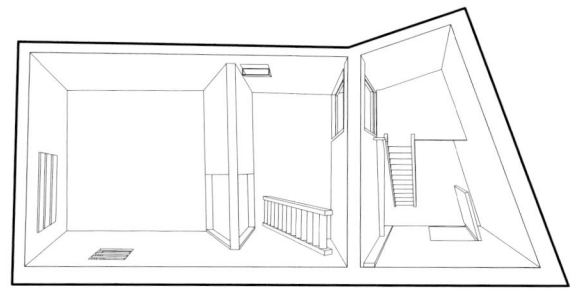

Plan perspectives

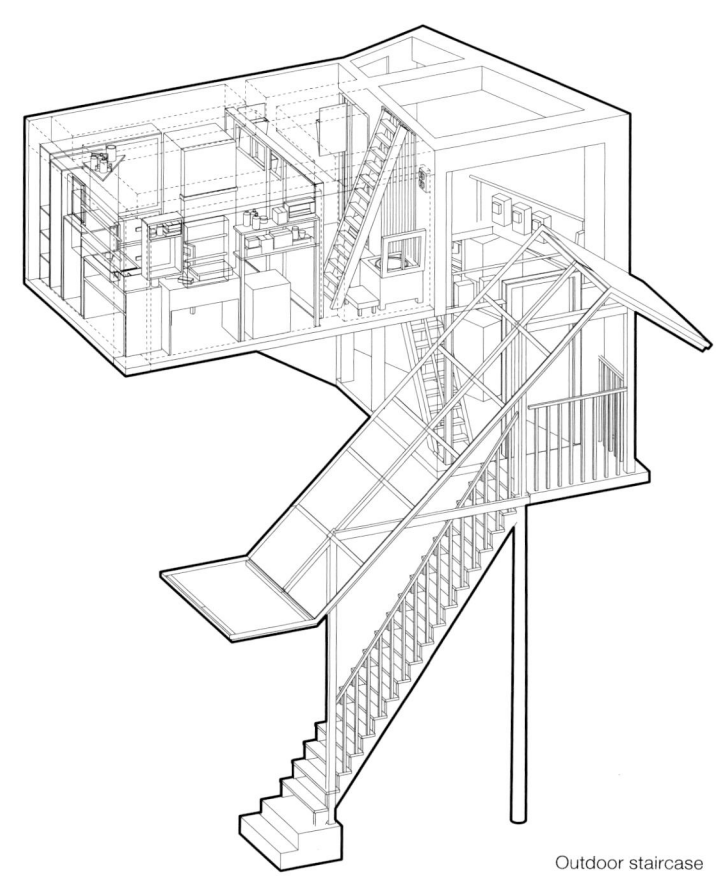

Outdoor staircase

Summer 2025

Home for a Veteran

Zhang Ming + Zhang Zi | Original Design Studio / TJAD

Location: Shantou Village, Pingdingshan City, Henan, China
Architect: Original Design Studio / TJAD
Principal architect: Zhang Ming, Zhang Zi
Site architect: Xi Weidong
Design team: Xi Weidong, Cao Kaiyi
Collaborator: Ubi (Shanghai) Building Technology Co. Ltd., Jimu Building Technology Engineering (Shanghai) Co. Ltd.
Construction: Pingdingshan Yatu Architecture and Furnishing Engineering Co. Ltd.
Gross floor area: 70 square meters
Design period: June 2018–July 2018
Completion: August 2018
Photography: Zhang Yong
Episode: *Dream House*, Season 5, Episode 1

This project was featured on the first episode of the fifth season of *Dream Home* in 2018. The project, located in Shantou Village, Pingdingshan City, Henan Province, renovates an old rammed-earth house of a 93-year-old veteran within a 15-day on-site construction time. The existing house had a leaky roof and had no sanitation facilities inside the house. The low ground was also prone to waterlogging. In addition to addressing these basic needs, the team also experimented with prefabricated modular units, modern steel-and-timber structures, and modern rammed-earth technology to meet the demanding time frame.

Existing house

Courtyard after renovation

This fast-track renovation aimed to offer the veteran an "old" house with warmth and memories, rather than simply build a brand-new house. The key was to preserve the traditional appearance of a small northern farmhouse and the memories of the veteran while improving and upgrading the functionality of the house within the tight deadline of 15 days of on-site construction. To completely retain the tiled roof and the southern rammed-earth wall, a nearly 7-meter-span beam was added to replace the rear load-bearing wall. As the rear wall was removed, prefabricated living room and bathroom modular units which were manufactured in a factory in Shanghai were inserted into the existing house by rails. To keep the comfortable height of the living space and to preserve the memory of the roof's past, the living room roof panel was designed in a herringbone pattern with clear triangular glass windows on the side to both visually increase the height of the house and to reveal the original roof and frame of the old house.

Following the traditional house layout, the northern part of the courtyard remains as the living area for the homeowner, while the southern part is designed as an activity area where elderly people and volunteers from the village can rest and chat with the veteran when they visit. A prefabricated reading room, as well as a leisure pavilion, is also placed here. The reading room module provides a space for the children of the village to read and play. The leisure pavilion module, together with the wooden benches and L-shaped connecting corridor, creates more space for leisure activities. As such, the renovated house is not only a new home for the veteran but also provides villagers and volunteers with additional activity spaces.

The biggest challenge on this project was time. Due to the limited construction time, the six modules had to be completed in the factory within 20 days to enable all construction finishes, including structural, plumbing, walling, and installation. This left only five days for the on-site construction as the rest of the construction process could only be carried out after the modules were in place. However, with the determination and combined efforts of the project's designers and construction team, the architects were able to complete the construction on time.

Outdoor pavilion

Inserted box volumes

View toward the courtyard

Wood veranda

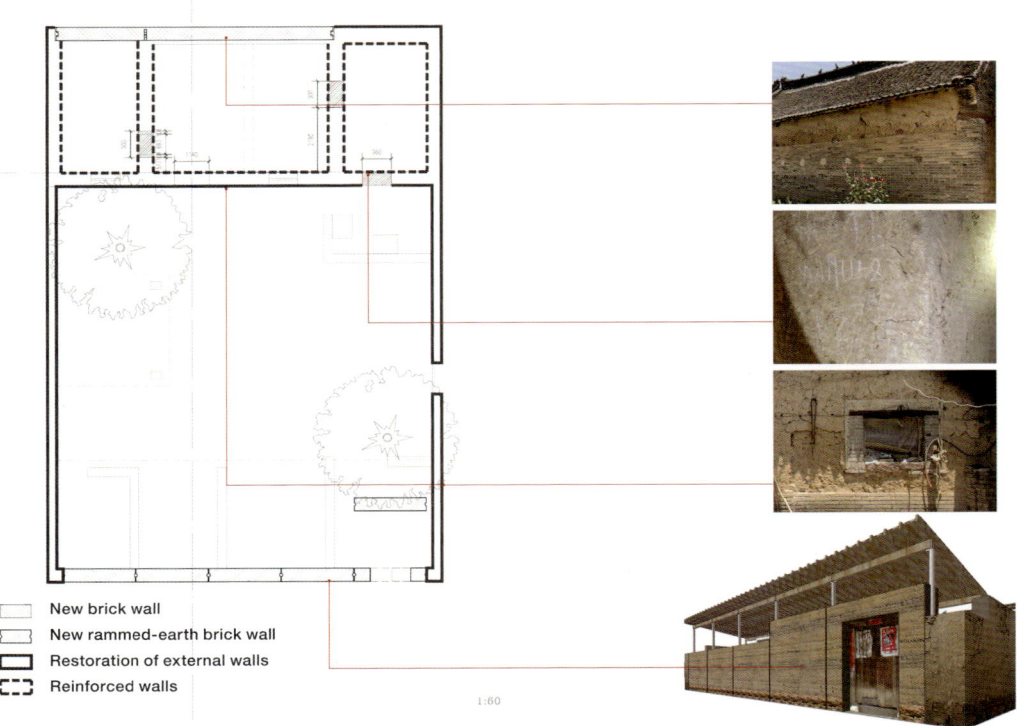

New brick wall
New rammed-earth brick wall
Restoration of external walls
Reinforced walls
1:60

Restoration drawing

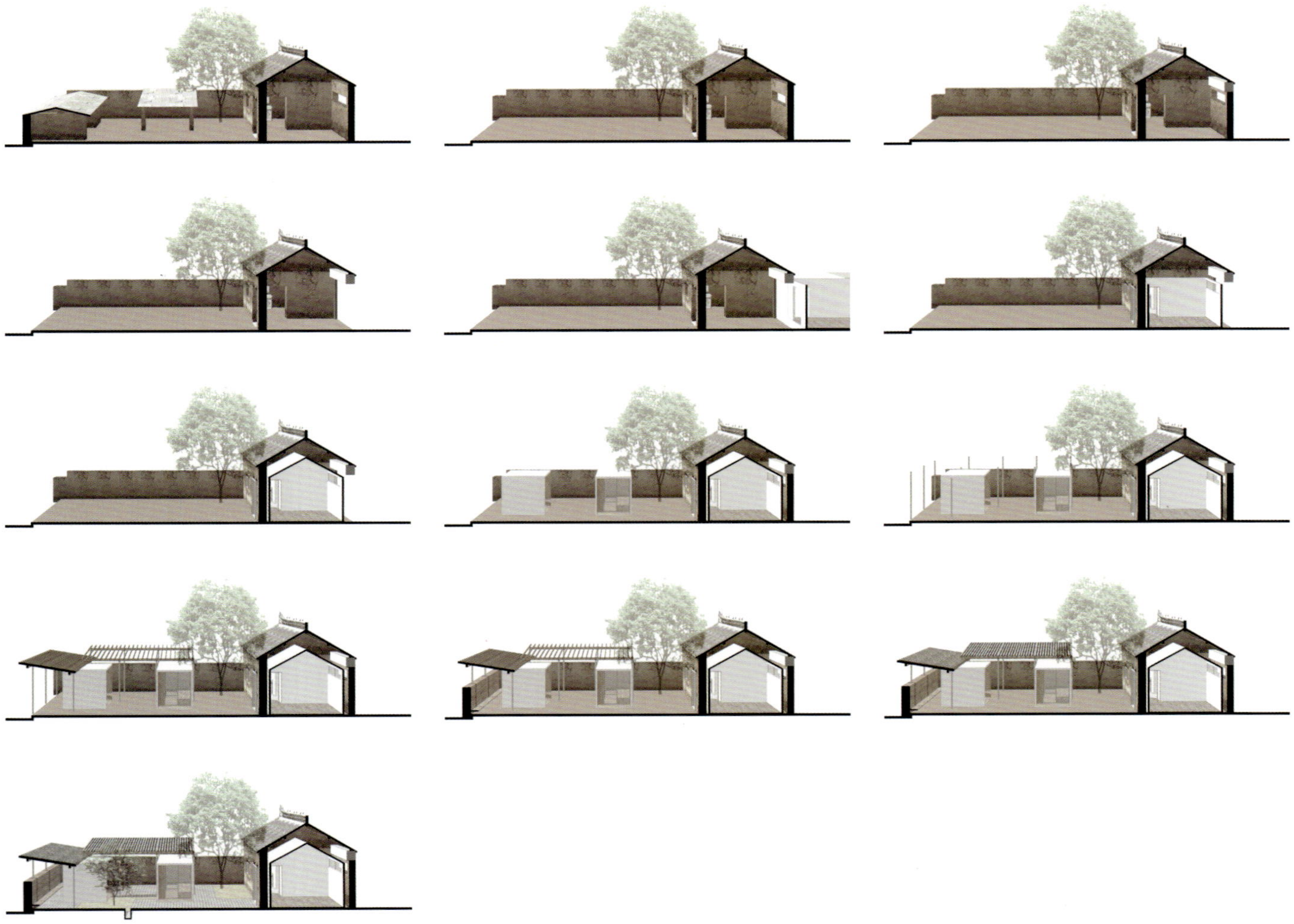

Renovation process

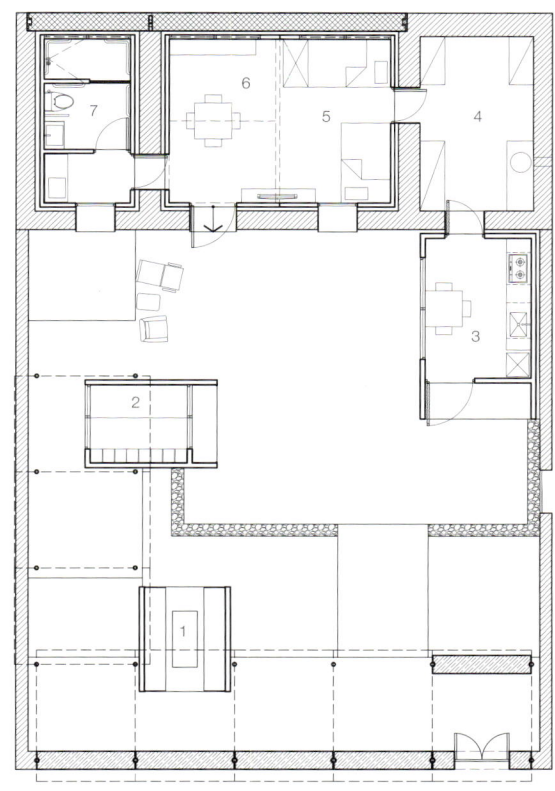

Plan

1. Open pavilion
2. Reading room
3. Kitchen
4. Storage room
5. Bedroom
6. Living room
7. Toilet

New rammed-earth wall
New brick wall
Retained existing walls

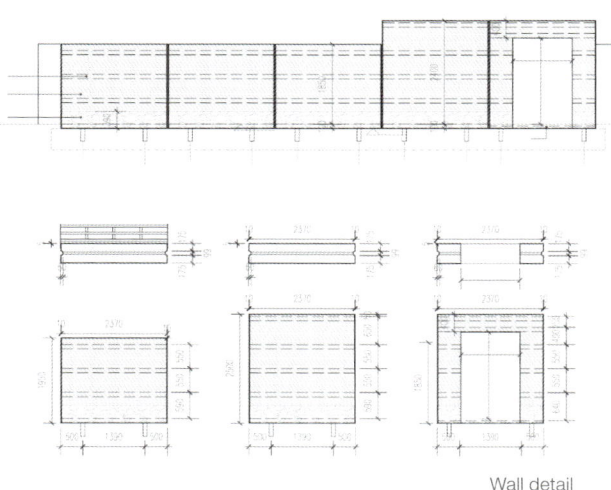

Wall detail

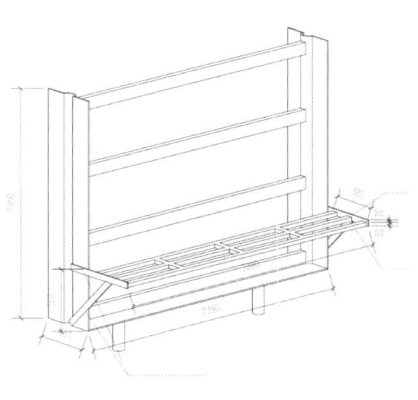

Bench detail

Summer 2025　23

The Instagram Archive of Aranya Holiday Resort: Image Creation Beyond the Camera Lens

Wang Xuerui
Assistant Professor, Tongji University

On July 7, 2014, an Instagram user named yao0403 posted on the social media platform the first photo of the sea and beach of a little-known resort in northern China, adding the hashtag #aranyaresort. Little did he know that just a year later, the empty space tagged in the photo, which most people had never heard of, would become one of the country's most famous tourist destinations after the spread of a viral video titled "The Loneliest Library in China." As of February 2021, the hashtag #aranyaresort yielded a total of 1,706 posts on Instagram. These posts stand as a visual archive of different users visiting the Aranya Holiday Resort. Before they were posted, these photos underwent the process of shooting to editing, selection, and the addition of descriptions to garner likes and comments on the platform, becoming a permanent part of the web that can still be traced to this day.

These hundreds of photos on Instagram barely scratch the surface and are inaccurate markers of the popularity of the Aranya Resort in China. As access to the platform is restricted on the Chinese mainland, its domestic users tend to be young people with a taste for new things, similar to hipsters in Western countries. While Chinese social media platforms like WeChat, the Twitter-like Weibo, and Douyin—as TikTok is not available in China—are popular with all ages in the country and host huge amounts of users and data, Instagram offers a novel outlet for young people in the Chinese mainland to express their identity. Yet, the users of this personalized medium are filtered by both means of access and the particular interests of this younger generation. With just a simple hashtag, for example #aranyaresort, the similarities in the day-to-day lives of these users are immediately made visible through Instagram's characteristic waterfall-like grid.

Susan Sontag once said, "To collect photographs is to collect the world." By analyzing the relevant tagged images on Instagram, many fascinating details can be observed, such as which buildings appear most frequently, and are there similarities between the photos taken by different people? In this article, I will use these 1,700 photos as a medium to identify the reasons why the Aranya Resort has become a viral Internet sensation and popular tourist spot, as well as the changes this has brought about. There are two main questions I wish to explore: First, how is the Aranya project presented through the camera lens? What angles are used, and which travel habits and environmental psychology are reflected in these photos? Second, and perhaps more importantly, how did the Aranya Resort acquire pop culture status beyond the camera? Which channels of communication were used? And further how should the relationship between architecture and capital be perceived when the former becomes apart of communication and the media?

Viral Architecture and the Tourism Real Estate Behind It

The Seashore Library That Went Viral on Social Media

On May 10, 2015, a promotional video for a "Lonely Library" went viral on social media, originally posted by the recently established WeChat account "Yitiao." Within just one day, the post had been viewed more than 100,000 times and garnered more than 4,000 likes, instantly turning the Seashore Library into a "viral architecture" sensation. In the video, the architect Dong Gong states that the library's design was inspired by modernist painter Andrew Wyeth's 1982 painting *Baleen*. The painting depicts an old man sitting by himself on a rock, with his back to the viewer as he looks out to the sea. Dong Gong expressed his belief that this painting embodies a lingering sense of loneliness. He said that through his design, he hopes to create the opportunity for everyone who comes to the library to "look at the sea as equals," and thus to reflect on themselves and their existence. The library accomplishes this vision with terraced seating in front of floor-to-ceiling windows facing the sea. Made of cast-in-situ fair-faced concrete, the rectangular volume stands entirely alone on the seashore, with daylight casting shadows across the building, creating imagery that evoke a sense of solitude. In order to underline this "loneliness," the video shows the library empty, with its exterior resembling the abandoned bunkers on the French coastline depicted in Paul Virilio's *Bunker Archaeology*. They stand in stoic defiance of the passage of time, embodied in the changing light and tides.

Shifting From Social Media to Trade Media

Soon after the "Lonely Library" became an Internet sensation, large crowds of visitors started flocking to the site, quickly exceeding the library's capacity, which can only accommodate a maximum of 3,000 people per day. In response, the library immediately set up an online reservation system, limiting access to 200 readers per day, but nevertheless, visitors continued to come in droves.

The architecture community was also part of this influx. But unlike the average visitor, the architects were more interested in the aesthetics of the building , taking it in more with a professional eye. Soon, ongoing critical discussions about the formal language of this "overnight sensation" arose. In the second half of 2015 alone, a total of six articles discussing the Seashore Library were published in three of China's leading architectural publications: *Architectural Journal*, *The Architect*, and *World Architecture*. Two of the articles were project descriptions authored by the architect himself; two were interviews or conversations between architects or scholars and Dong Gong; and the other two were academic commentaries on the Seashore Library. Given the context of the articles, we can discern that Dong Gong did not just want to hand over his work to popular culture, but to also include it in serious, orthodox, academic discussions within architecture circles. Interestingly, in these essays, the architect no longer used the words "solitude" or "loneliness" to describe the atmosphere of the library, but instead employed architectural terminology, like site, space, structure, section, and material to explain his creation.

Capitalism Through Architecture: A Safety Pin for Tourism Real Estate?

The Seashore Library belongs to the Aranya Holiday Resort in Beidaihe New District, Hebei Province. This background is often overlooked, yet it is a prerequisite to explaining many questions. The Aranya Resort forms part of the larger Aranya Gold Coast Community located in Changli County, Qinhuangdao City, approximately 40 kilometers from downtown Qinhuangdao and 300 kilometers from downtown Beijing. A tourism real estate project, the resort complex covers a total area of 2.2 square kilometers and carries a 40-year land lease agreement. In 2015, the Aranya Resort started gaining public awareness due to the successful marketing of the "Lonely Library." Since then, the developer has been cooperating with a series of famous domestic architectural firms to create distinctive buildings for the community, including the Seashore Chapel (Dong Gong, Vector Architects), the Dune Museum (Li Hu & Huang Wenjing, OPEN Architecture Studio), and the Aranya Art Center (Lyndon Neri & Rossana Hu, Neri&Hu Design and Research Office). Bolstered by community events, the increased popularity has driven up real estate prices and sales, transforming the Aranya Resort from a "dying real estate project" in 2012 to a virtual "real estate miracle." This may sound like a Chinese version of the "Bilbao effect." However, unlike the positive contribution of the Guggenheim Museum Bilbao to the Spanish city's development, the role of architecture as an accessory to upgrade a real estate project does not seem to reflect the priority of the architects involved. Compared to the bourgeois vibe that the Aranya Resort intends to create, the architects seem to favor a complex architectural, artistic, and phenomenological vocabulary in an effort to move the architecture to the cultural, aesthetic, and spiritual end of the discussion spectrum.

The architecture of the Aranya Resort seems to integrate two extremes: the "pure form" made possible by the liberal creative environment provided to the architects, and the cultural symbols that attract tourists and homebuyers to this viral photo spot. According to Manfredo Tafuri's theory, modernist architecture began as a revolt against capitalism and the aesthetics of the bourgeoisie, while the collusion of the avant-garde with the moneyed elite would eventually lead to its gradual demise. But the community buildings at the Aranya Resort exist precisely for the purpose of attracting consumers. Like shiny safety pins holding together a real estate portfolio, they provide utopian sceneries for the cultural and aesthetic taste that the middle class strives to embody. Therefore, the part played by these "modern buildings" for a real estate project may not be compatible with the claimed cultural purpose behind their form, and this is perhaps also the reason why the architects tend to replace the discussion of the project's social values with statements about its perceptual experience and so on.

The Importance of Images in Aranya's Media Communication

Instagrammable Architecture

If we take another look at the 1,700 photos of the Aranya Resort on Instagram, we quickly notice a somewhat surprising phenomenon: the majority of the images that include buildings feature the Seashore Chapel of the Aranya Resort, rather than the more famous and older Seashore Library. Why is that? Analyzing this from the perspective of photographic composition, the rationale is that most visitors used their mobile phone cameras that usually allow a focal length of 23–50 millimeters to take their photos, thereby making it difficult to capture the library's horizontal volume in its entirety without lens distortion. So, the photographs with the library as the main feature are more likely to only use parts of the building as a frame or background. In comparison, the Seashore Chapel is smaller in volume, and photos can often include panoramic views of the building, the beach, and the sea in one single frame. Additionally, its triangular volume is more unusual and the symmetrical vertical composition has a stronger iconic effects. Also, characteristic elements such as the spire, stairs, and the building's nameplate stand out, enticing visitors to take photos.

On social media, viral architecture is often depicted from similar angles and with similar compositions. Most of these photos are taken from specific vantage points or locations that allow for the best visual effect. Artist Felice Varini's public art installation acts as a suitable metaphor for this approach to photography. The spatial imagery of seemingly two-dimensional and three-dimensional elements is closely linked to the observer's point of view. In his installation, the artist projected a laser from a specific position into the space and marked its contour with paint, so that an observer can only see the full image if he or she stands in the exact same position as the original laser projector. As soon as the position or angle deviates from it, only irregular color fragments are visible.

In spaces where the primary purpose is to take photographs, viewers often don't care about issues such as their comfort, sustainability, or practicality—photographic beauty is the only thing that matters to them. In other words, photographs conceal a range of information about the site, materials, and function of the building. Regarding this loss of information, Robin Evans once discussed the reverse of this topic in his essay titled "Translations from Drawings to Building." In his view, a two-dimensional drawing is a "translation" of a three-dimensional building, which means that this image may hide, enhance, and change people's actual perception of the built architecture, resulting in a loss of information and misalignment between the two. Evans mainly discusses the process from drawings to buildings, but we can find that the same unequal relationship also applies to the reproduction of buildings in images, for example, photographs of viral architecture. The transition from drawing to building and back to an image forms a closed loop of "design-construction-use," also known as the creation and consumption of architecture. However, within this process, the focus of media communication on visual images places the consumption of architecture at an equal level with its creation, and in some cases even above the meaning of architectural creation.

Artworks in the Age of Digital Reproduction

Through their dissemination via social media, carefully designed sceneries and beautiful images become expressions of their publisher's identity and aesthetic taste, quickly attracting more people to the same spot who seek the same angle to shoot the same scene. Just like in Felice Varini's installation, every spectator strives to recreate the "perfect" geometric shape by emulating the artist's original projection and precisely adjusting their shooting position and posture. We might name this act of photographic repetition amplified by the circulation on the Internet "digital reproduction."

In the 1930s, Walter Benjamin argued in his book *The Work of Art in the Age of Mechanical Reproduction* that the exhibition value of modern visual art—characterized by its mechanical reproducibility—would replace the cult value of traditional art, and that the rise of mass media would allow more and more people to participate in the creation of art. Benjamin thus asks how we should understand the authenticity of the works we see in magazine photographs, postcards, and films. What is the meaning of the artwork when viewed outside its cultural context of creation? At that time, Benjamin used the term "here and now" of an artwork as a definition of its "authenticity." Almost a century later, the dissemination speed of information has been further accelerated by the Internet, while convenient forms of mobility have greatly reduced the time required to cross physical distances, allowing people to quickly reach the location of an artwork and to recreate and redistribute its picture through social media. However, the reduction in information and physical distance does not seem to have led to a return to "authenticity." Instead, these media representations firmly tie the techniques of creating powerful images to the consumer's desire for and the illusion of a "good life," contributing to their belief that consumption is solely about aesthetics.

This is obviously not the case. Behind the online propagation of images of the Aranya Resort lies a set of complex factors involving socioeconomic, capitalist, and crowd psychology dynamics. Sociologist Sharon Zukin once argued that urban change requires a combination of politico-economic and sociocultural analyses, incorporating four main elements: capital, real estate, media preferences, and consumer preferences. This argument suggests that we need to look at the implications of Aranya's architecture in the context of urban development. As part of a real estate project, the community architecture of the Aranya Resort can be considered a prime example of successfully channeling consumer preferences through media communication at the hands of capital. Many scholars have used sociologist Pierre Bourdieu's theoretical framework of "field" and "capital" to explain viral architecture and the Aranya Resort as tourism real estate, a vacation community, an artistic brand, and a promotional subject can be considered a "field." Between investors, homeowners, tourists, and the broader potential clientele, the Aranya Resort establishes the power structure of the urban middle class through media projections of art and culture. The balance of power and the competition between the different actors is based on capital as the goal and the means to achieve a "win-win" situation for all stakeholders by accumulating not only economic, but also cultural and social capital.

Pictorial Feedback as Post-Occupancy Evaluation for Architecture

In a 2019 interview published in the architecture and design magazine *Domus*, Dutch architecture firms UNstudio and OMA/AMO discussed the possible impact of Instagram on architecture, even going so far as to explore the potential use of social media apps to monitor the use and experience of a building once it is completed. According to OMA/AMO architect Giacomo Ardesio, "The more a building is capable of engaging somehow the visitors beyond the program that it is meant to solve, at least from a certain point of view, the more it is successful today." Ardesio's opinion reveals the dissociation between the actual use of contemporary architecture and its intended function. Let's take Aranya Holiday Resort's Seashore Chapel as an example. Architect Dong Gong described it in his article for *World Architecture* as follows: "The Seashore Chapel is a spiritual space within the community where people contemplate, listen to their inner voices, and experience the beauty of a single ray of light. It is also a place where cultural events and art exhibitions are held. It is a cultural and artistic space imbued with a strong sense of art." The first half of this description may stand as slightly inaccurate as the majority of the general public is not allowed to enter the chapel. Only Aranya's property owners and residents, as well as a handful of visitors with admission vouchers are allowed to enter the church. Though, considering the chapel alongside David Harvey's criticism of the "privatization of public space," at least in everyday life, the functional vision for its interior has almost completely yielded to the "unintended" behavior of taking pictures of its exterior space. As a community space with the formal layout of a wedding chapel, the white triangular spire and the sea-facing interior are very evocative of beautiful wedding imagery. However, when we take a closer look with a more critical eye, we will notice that light mainly enters the chapel from the seaside. If a wedding were to be held here, the ceremony itself can only be photographed against the light, rendering the ideal wedding scene as merely a figment of one's imagination.

In the latter part of his description, Dong Gong defines the building as "a place where cultural events and art exhibitions are held," yet more often than not, it is the exterior space of the building that is used as a temporary venue for events, for instance, the Aranya Community Children's Fashion Show during summer. Initiated by the visitor-users themselves, the temporary use of the space, which can be considered an innovative spatial type, creates a distinctive local identity that becomes its own marketing brand due to the site, its inhabitants, and the media coverage of the activities. Thus, in the context of the post-occupancy evaluation of architecture, media not only plays an important role in providing opportunities for cultural consumption, but also in the reproduction of culture. As far as the contemporary media environment is concerned, the creation of architecture in which people are willing to stay and realize behaviors beyond its predetermined function stands as proof of its success. Yet, only if the quality of architecture is assessed in terms of the actual use of a space, rather than simply the content of media images alone, will architecture be able to keep its meaning and construct a living world where richness and authenticity coexist.

Seashore Library

Dong Gong | Vector Architects

Location: Aranya Gold Coast Community, Beidaihe New District, Qinhuangdao, Hebei Province, China
Architect: Vector Architects
Principal architect: Dong Gong
Project architect: Chen Liang
Site architect: Zhang Yifan, Sun Dongping
Design team: Liu Zhiyong, Hsi Chao Chen, Hsi Mei Hsieh
Structural and MEP engineering: Beijing Yanhuang International Architecture & Engineering Co., Ltd.
Structural consultant: Ji Lixin, Liu Zhongyu
Gross floor area: 450 square meters
Design period: February–July 2014
Construction period: July 2014–April 2015
Photography: Su Shengliang, Xia Zhi, He Bin

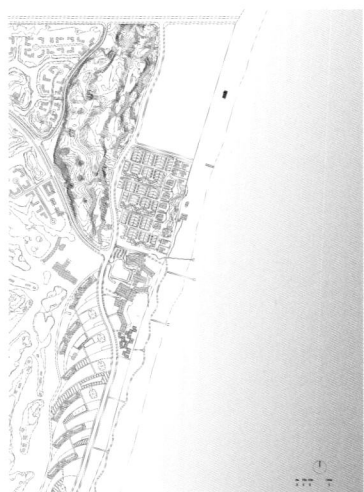

Site plan

About a three-hour drive from Beijing, the Seashore Library is located inside the Aranya vacation compound along the coastline of Bohai Bay. With rapid urban development, the decline in the quality of the living environment in Beijing has become an increasing problem. This resort community aims to provide residents with version of a high-quality life that is life close to nature and which offers a range of cultural and recreational facilities, of which the Seashore Library is one.

The main concept of the design is to explore the coexistence of the boundaries of space and physical activity, changes in light and atmosphere, air circulation, and views of the sea. Facing the sea on the east side, the library serves the community of the western settlement in spring, summer, and autumn, and is open to the public free of charge.

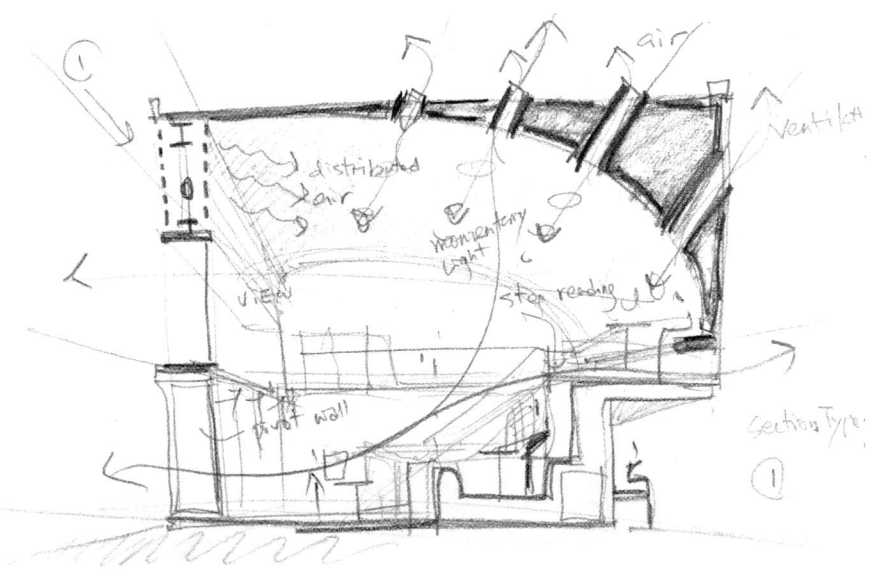

Dong Gong's sketch

Seashore Library by the Bohai Bay © Su Shengliang

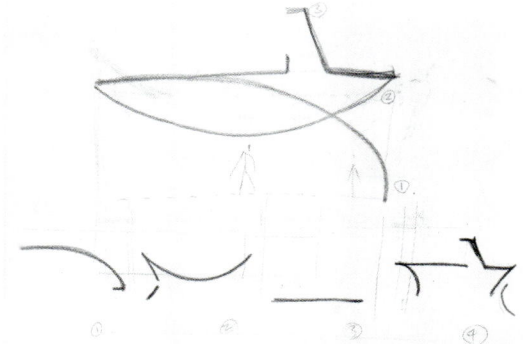

Dong Gong's sectional study sketch

Seashore Library has been described "the most solitary library in China" © Su Shengliang

The interior lighting rendering the concrete volumes translucent at night © Xia Zhi

The design of the library began by reflecting on the section. The library is made up of a main reading space, a meditation space, an activity room, and a small water bar lounge. We set the specific relationship between the spaces and the sea and defined the way in which light and wind enter each space based on its functional needs.

The sea, in all its diversity, evolves with the change of seasons and the flow of time, like an unfolding plot of a nature-themed drama. The main program, the reading space, is conceptualized as a "grandstand," iterated as gradually rising platforms that provides unobstructed views of the sea from different positions inside the building. On the seaward side, the ground floor features a movable "wall" made up entirely of glass revolving doors. In good weather, this "wall" is completely opened, creating a more direct, intimate relationship between the library interior and the sea. An horizontal window that spans across the space above the glass "wall" offers a view toward the sea and is the focal point of the entire space. To avoid visual interference, the roof load is supported entirely by the steel trusses above the window. The trusses are flanked on both the inside and outside by translucent walls made of hand-burned glass blocks. Sensitive to light, the translucence of the walls showcases the inside and outside of the building in different hues and light atmospheres at different times of the day.

The curved roof opens out toward the sea, underscoring and solidifying the theme of the space, while the curved lines contribute to the large span of the roof structure in both the east–west and north–south dimensions. The 30-centimeter-diameter ventilation shafts on the roof can be opened and closed electrically when the weather permits, further driving the flow of the interior space. During spring, summer, and autumn, from around 1 pm to 4 pm, sunlight penetrates these narrow air ducts and casts slow, wandering light speckles across the space.

Concrete rooftop © Su Shengliang

Reading area facing the sea © He Bin

Terraced platforms in the reading lounge © He Bin

Curved roof and horizontal window © Xia Zhi

Skylight bringing out light and darkness to add depth
© Xia Zhi

Skylight and sapce © Su Shengliang

The meditation space is located to the side of the reading space. In contrast to the bright, homogeneous, open, and public reading space, this space is dark, clearly lit, closed, and intimate. A 30-centimeter-wide slit at the east and west ends of the space connects to the outside. One slit is horizontal, while the other is vertical, through which the sun casts sundial-like beams of light in the morning and at dusk. The recessed roof further reduces the scale of the space, while the concave shape forms an outdoor terraced space above. Here, one can hear the sound of the waves but cannot see the sea.

The activity room is a relatively isolated space, separated from the reading space by an outdoor terrace in consideration of potential noise disruptions. The east-facing skylight on the roof and the high side windows in the west wall receive light from different directions at different times of the day, allowing a

View toward the reading lounge through a wall opening © Xia Zhi

simultaneous overlap of warm and cool light to be projected in the space.

If the building were to be dissected along its long north–south axis, it becomes clear that each space interprets a specific relationship with the sea. The movement of the human body through space and memory subliminally links these relationships to create a conscious experience.

Framed view of the sea © Su Shengliang

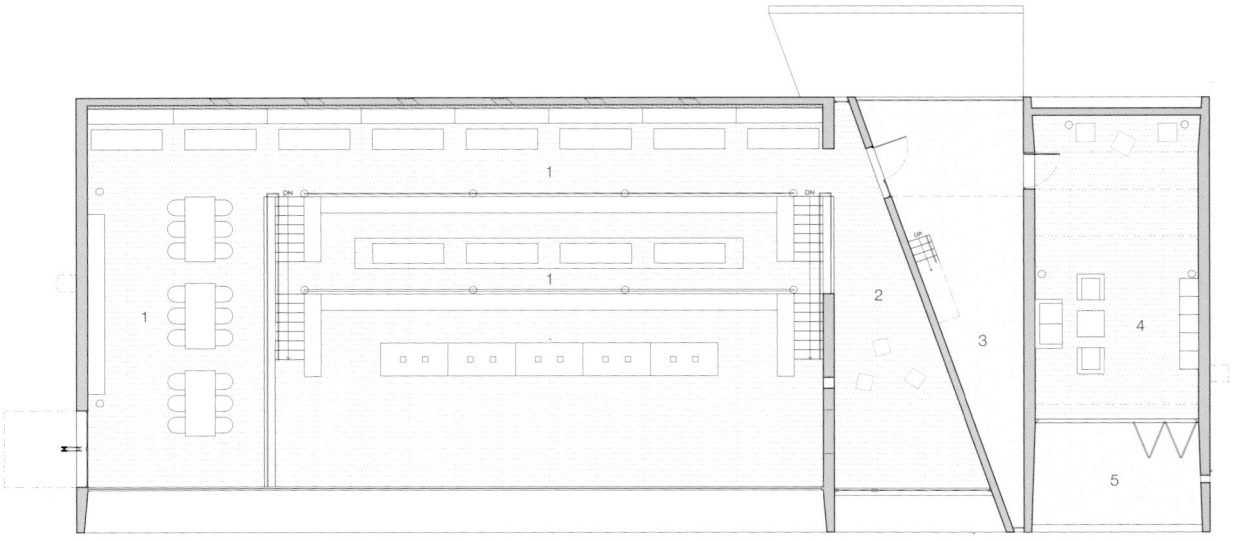

Second-floor plan

1. Reading area
2. Meditation space
3. Outdoor platform
4. Activity room
5. Balcony

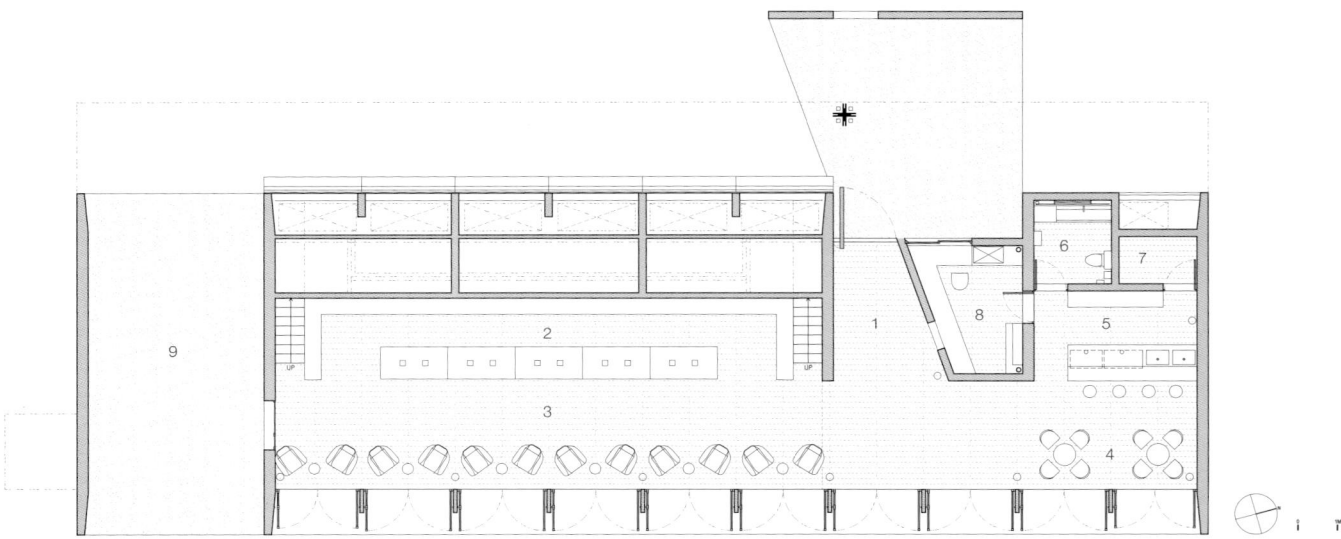

First-floor plan

1. Reception
2. Book display area
3. Reading lounge
4. Resting area
5. Water bar
6. Restroom
7. Storage
8. Office
9. Outdoor area

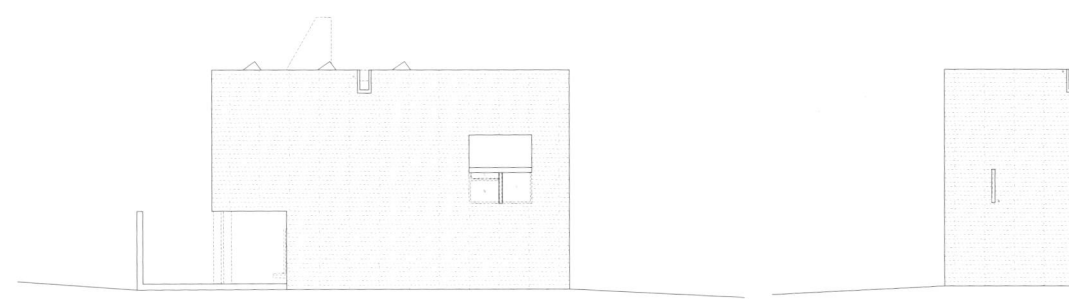

West elevation

East elevation

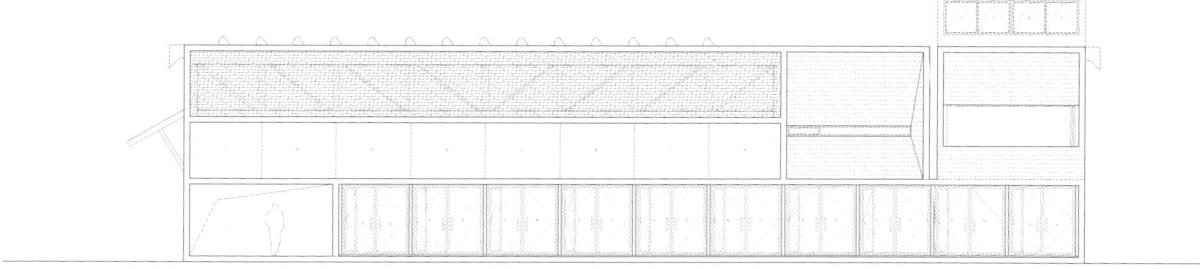

South elevation

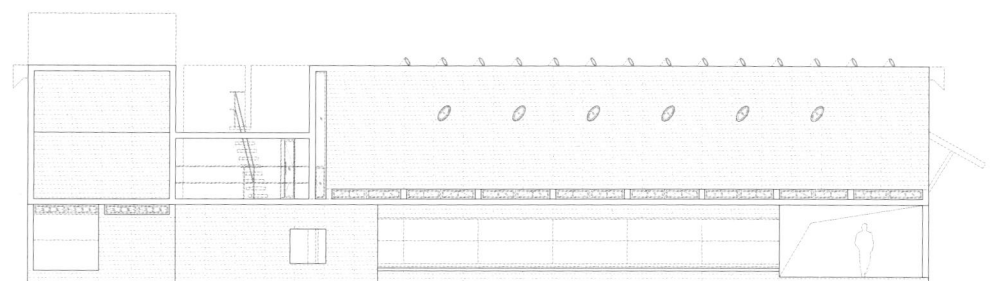

North elevation

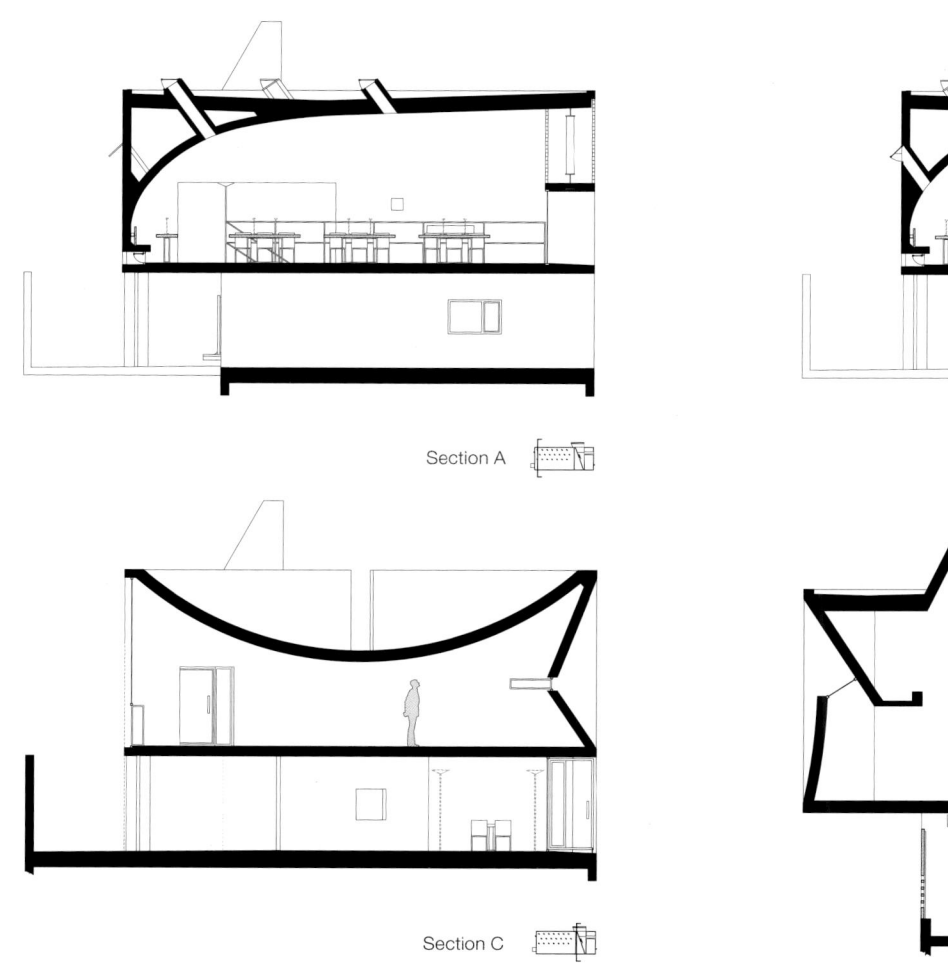

Section A

Section B

Section C

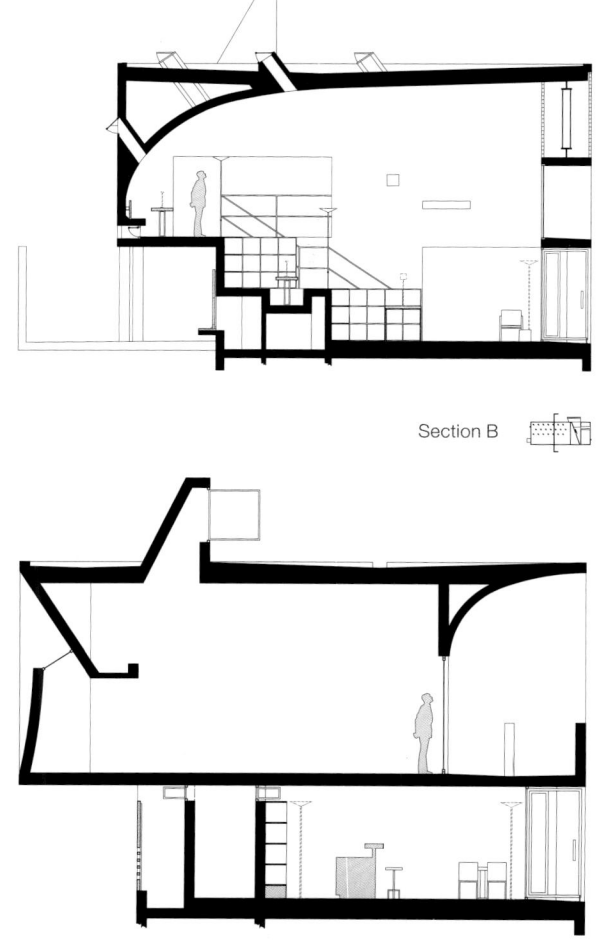

Section D

Summer 2025 35

Detail

1. Aluminum-frame electrical awning window: gray fluorocarbon coated
2. Cast-in-place wood-formed concrete
3. Air cavity
4. Bar light
5. 40 mm wooden bamboo plate
6. 20 mm wooden bamboo plate
7. 10x10 mm drip edge
8. Wooden bamboo-frame electrical awning window: ultra-clear glass
9. Steel column: painted black in flat matte
10. 50 mm wooden bamboo plate
11. Wooden bamboo flooring
12. Waterproof concrete roof

Detail

1. Cast-in-place wood-formed concrete
2. 10x10 mm drip edge
3. Wooden bamboo-frame side hung door: ultra-clear glass (swing out)
4. Wooden bamboo-frame side hung door: ultra-clear glass (swing in)
5. Reinforced fine aggregate concrete floor
6. Wooden bamboo flooring

Detail

1. Wooden bamboo-frame electrical casement window: ultra-clear glass (swing out)
2. Cast-in-place wood-formed concrete
3. Wooden bamboo-frame fixed window: ultra-clear glass
4. 10x10 mm drip edge
5. Wooden bamboo-frame casement window: ultra-clear glass (swing out)
6. 900x2075x20 mm mirror
7. Cast-in-place concrete sink
8. Wooden bamboo flooring

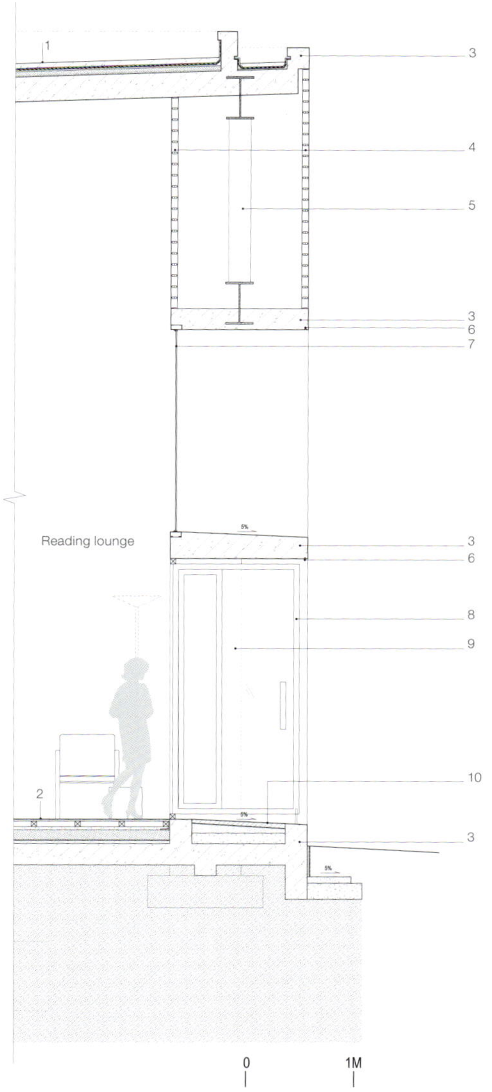

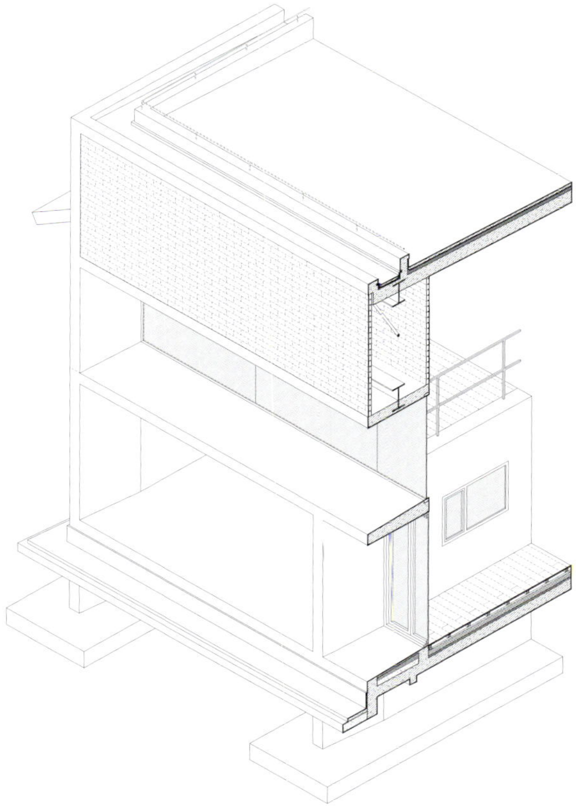

1
3
4
5
3
6
7
Reading lounge
3
6
8
9
10
2
3
0
1M

Detail

1. Waterproof concrete roof
2. Wooden bamboo flooring
3. Cast-in-place wood-formed concrete
4. Air bubble-filled handcrafted glass blocks
5. Steel trusses: gray fluorocarbon coated
6. 10x10 mm drip edge
7. Ultra-clear tempered glass
8. Wooden bamboo-frame side hung door: ultra-clear glass
9. Concrete structural column
10. Reinforced fine aggregate concrete floor

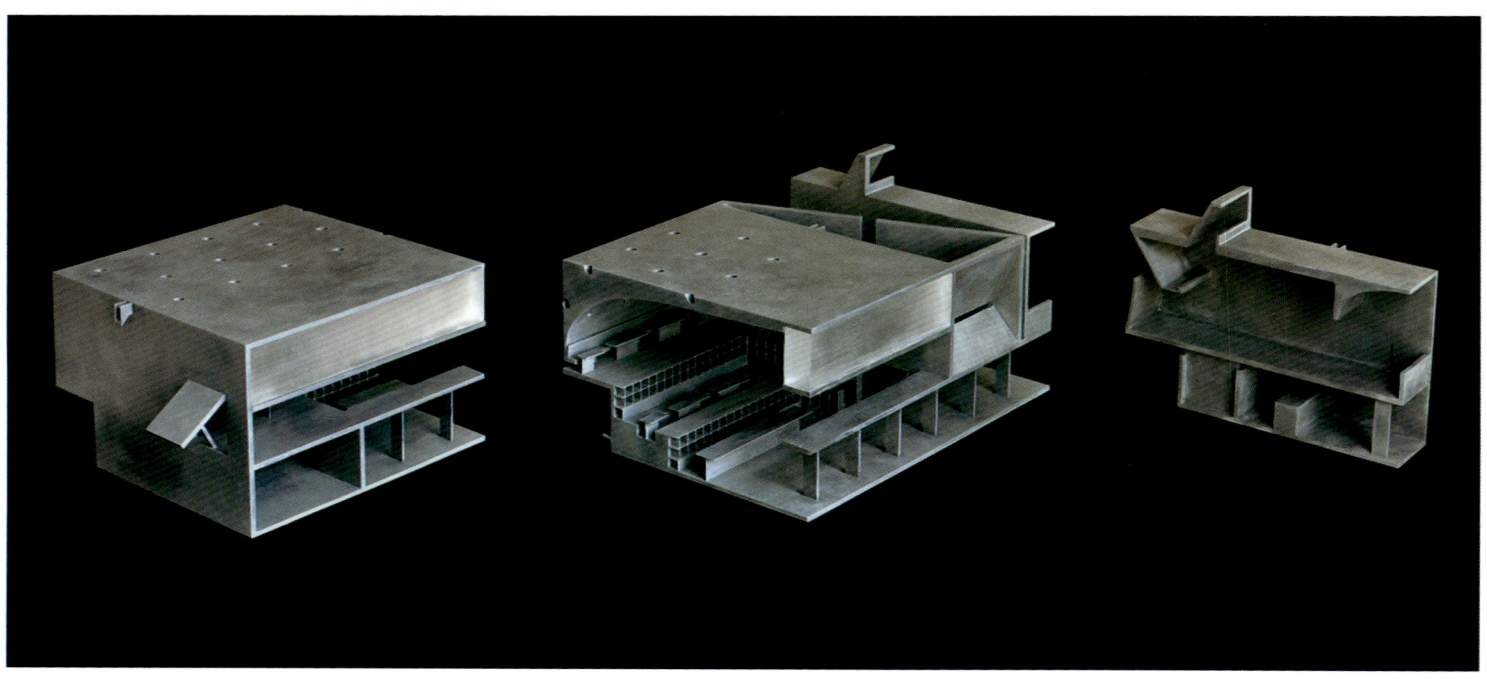

Sectional model

Seashore Chapel

Dong Gong | Vector Architects

Location: Aranya Gold Coast Community, Beidaihe New District, Qinhuangdao, Hebei Province, China
Architect: Vector Architects
Principal architect: Dong Gong
Project architect: Sun Dongping
Site architect: Sun Dongping
Design team: Yi Chi Wang, Liu Zhiyong, Zhang Yifan
Structural and MEP engineering: Beijing Yanhuang International Architecture & Engineering Co., Ltd.
Structural consultant: Ji Lixin, Liu Zhongyu
Gross floor area: 270 square meters
Design period: August–November 2014
Construction period: November 2014–October 2015
Photography: Chen Hao, Shi Zheng

Site plan

The chapel is imagined as a ship that once drifted on the sea, a long time ago. As the years passed and the waters receded, an elevated structure is left on the beach.

The elevated design creates two types of life. The lower level is a covered seafront space that provides shelter from the rain and sun for people on the beach. From the architects' perspective, it is more a space that is connected with secular community life. Because the chapel is so close to the sea, during high tide this space may even be submerged by the sea, and at that moment, the building is an imaginary ship once again. The upper floor is a space that belongs to the religion. As one approaches it, through a 600-millimeter gap in the middle of the large steps leading to the the upper floor, one can faintly perceive the lower level and glimpse a small section of the horizon. One walks up the stairs, enters the door, goes around the shadow wall, and finally enters a church space facing the sea. One beholds only the endless sea as the space is elevated, removing from the line of sight the beach or the people on it.

The opening to the outside world is minimal, allowed only through the large, horizontal, transparent window at the bottom of the space facing the sea. To prevent the area from becoming too bright, the large sea-facing windows are lowered to a height of 2.7 meters, placing only the sea within one's line of sight. The interior of the church at a height of 10 meters is enveloped in muted, intimate atmosphere. Natural light seeps into the interior through gaps in the walls, including a triangular skylight above the altar. The chapel's pointed, sloping roof acts as another channel of light.

The narrow 300-millimeter-long gap between the curved, inwardly curving wall on the south side and the north wall allows natural light to seep into the space from the top. During the three seasons of spring, summer, and autumn, when the angle of sun height is sufficiently vertical, the midday sun pours down the north wall, creating a moving but fleeting light atmosphere. When that happens, the concave and convex texture of the stucco walls is magnified to the extreme by the light, like skin that can be touched.

On the north side of the space is a meditation space that teeters outward. The scale of the space allows only one person within it at any given time. The walls on either side are tightly wedged around the human body, giving way to a curved wall that swirls away toward the sea, drawing the eye to the distant horizon.

Aerial view © Shi Zheng

Seashore Chapel at night © Chen Hao

Seashore Chapel against the backdrop of Bohai Bay © Chen Hao

The design takes full account of natural ventilation. In order to maintain the closed image of the chapel, the glass windows for light and ventilation are concealed between the building volumes and the parallel outside walls.

The Seashore Chapel serves the resort community to its west and is the furthest human-made space in the complex that reaches out to sea. In addition to the use of this space by religious worshippers, a great deal of community public activity will also take place here. Both the chapel and the Seashore Library, just 300 meters away, compose a set of spiritual places on the beach where one can quiet the mind, experience nature, and feel oneself.

Elevated area and platform © Chen Hao

40   Architecture China

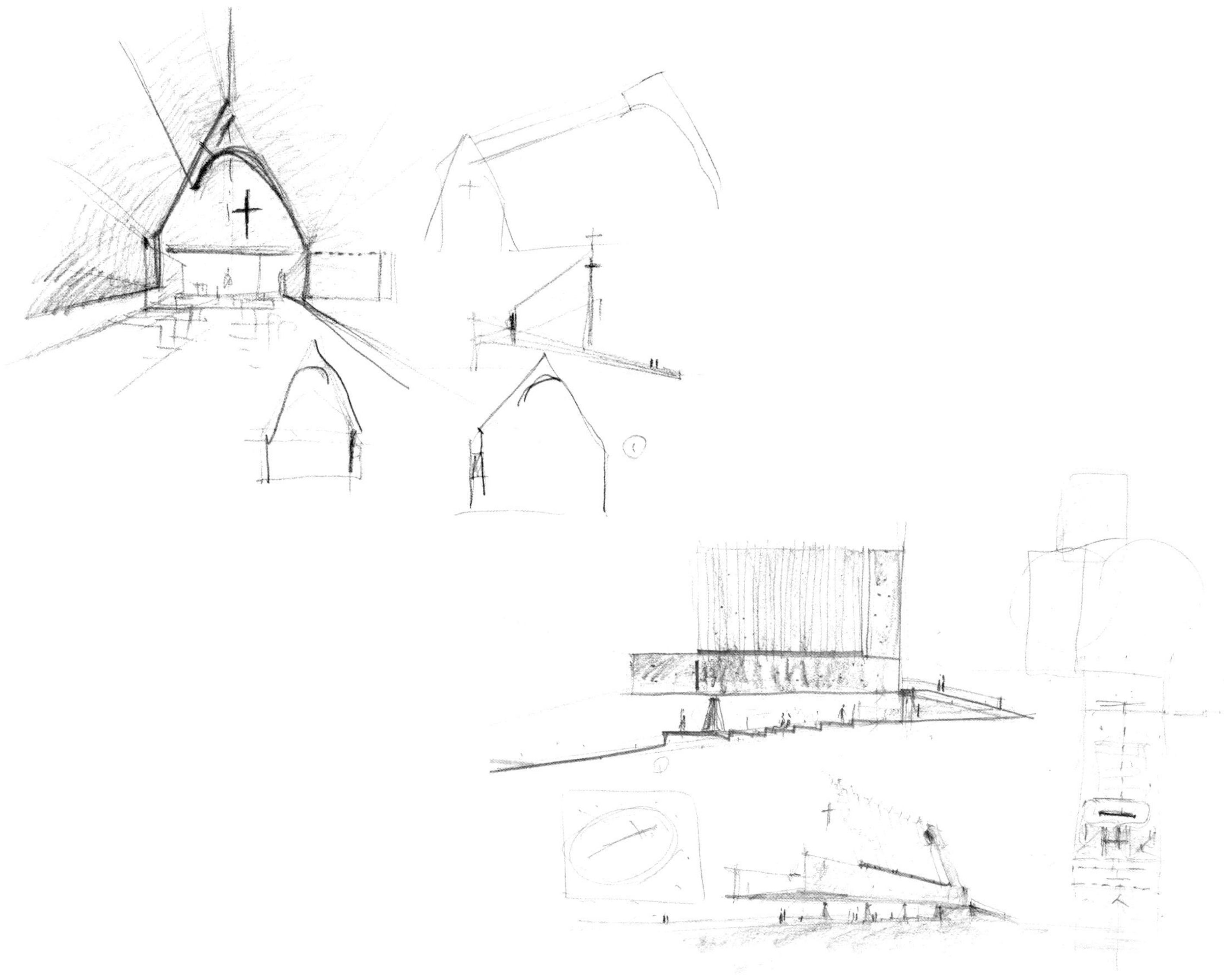

Dong Gong's conceptual sketches

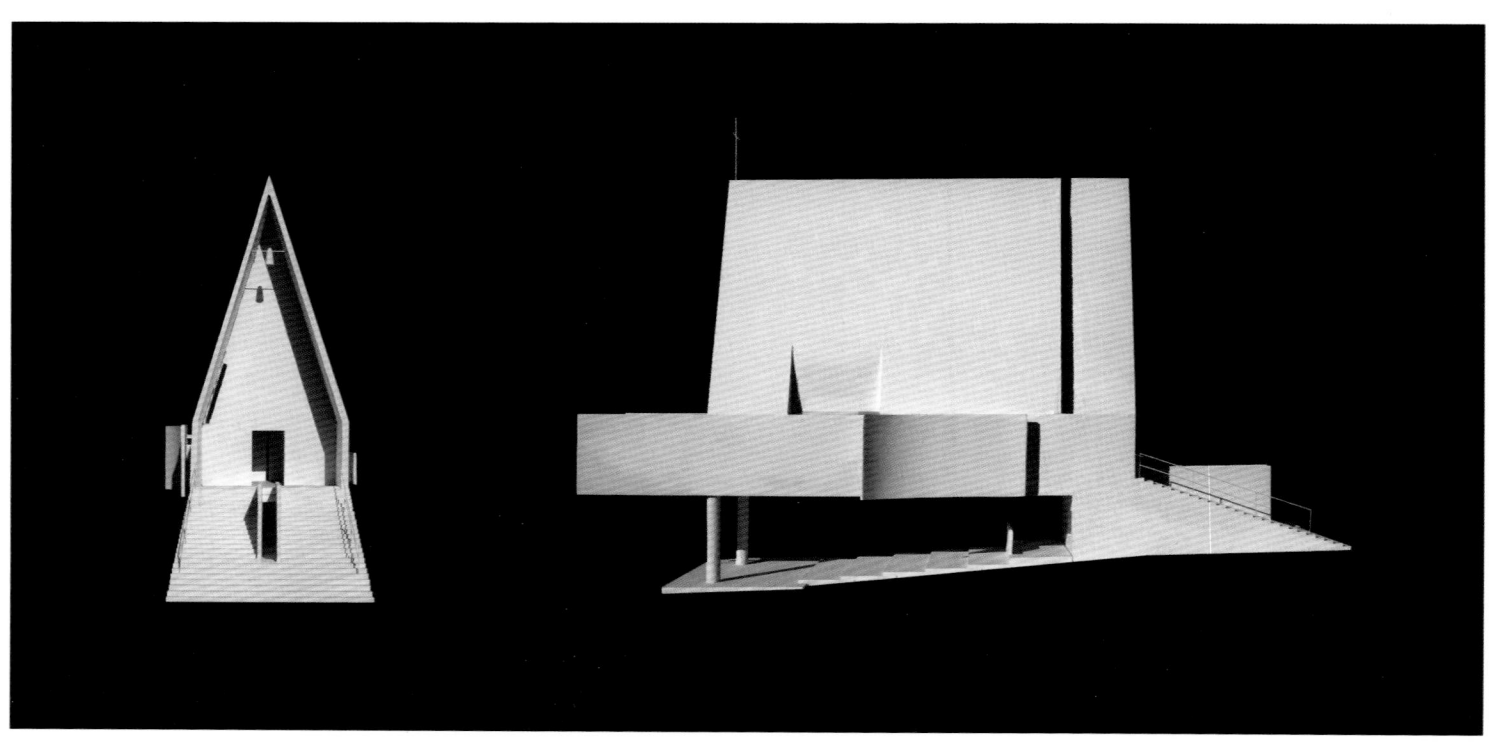

Model

Multiple skylights create an ethereal interior atmosphere © Chen Hao

Light in different hues through a colored glass skylight © Chen Hao

Entrance © Chen Hao

42 Architecture China

Auditorium facing the sea © Chen Hao

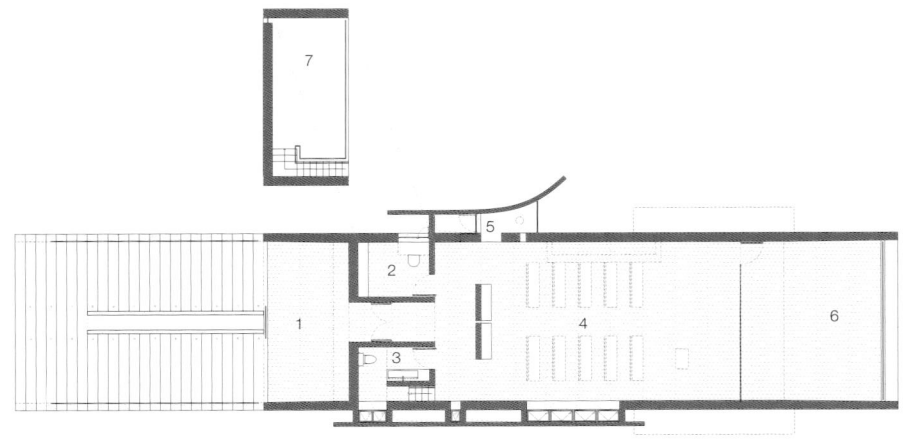

Second-floor plan

1. Entrance platform
2. Office
3. Restroom
4. Auditorium
5. Meditation space
6. Balcony
7. Piano room

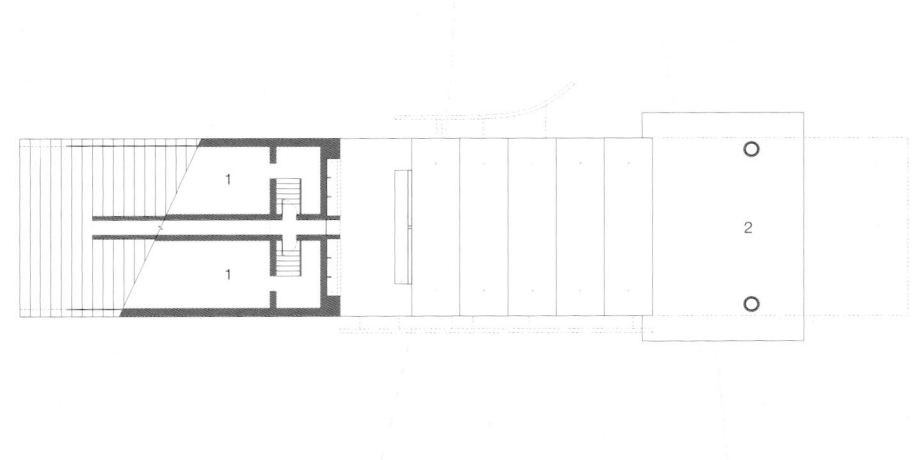

First-floor plan

1. Storage
2. Ocean-viewing platform

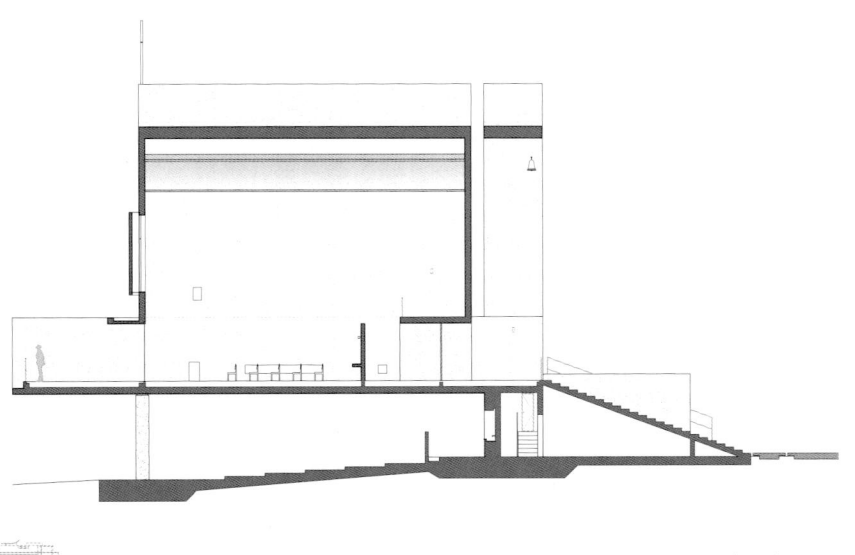

Longitudinal section

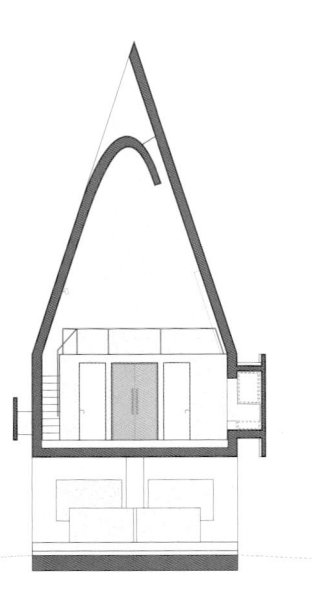

Profile section

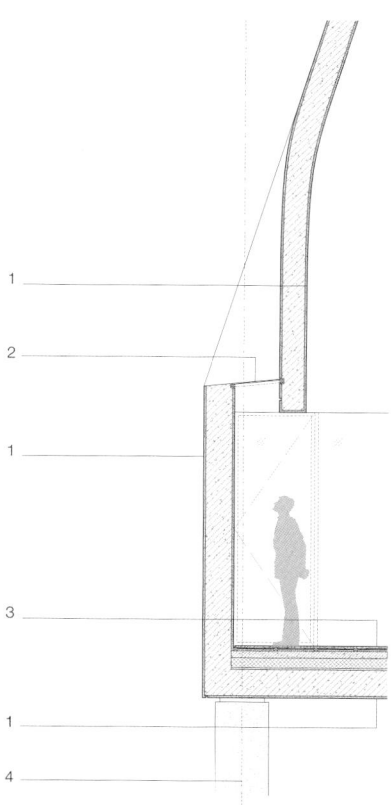

Detail

1. White stucco
2. 10 mm ultra-clear tempered glass
3. Laminated bamboo flooring
4. φ500 mm steel column with 50 mm concrete cover

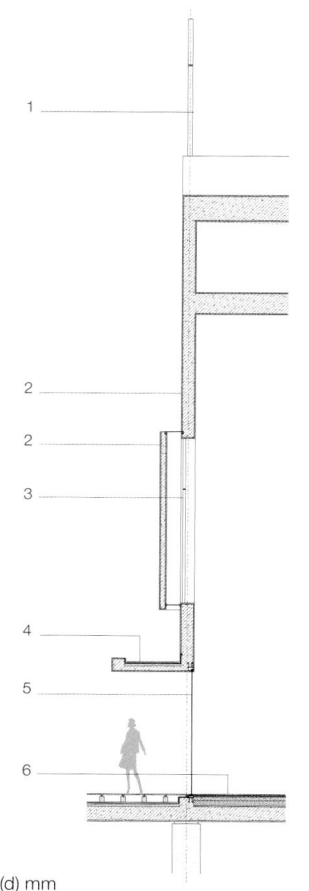

Detail

1. Brass cross 30 (w)x100 (d) mm
2. White stucco
3. Brass cross 20 (w)x60 (d) mm
4. White pebble stone
5. 15 mm ultra-clear tempered glass
6. Laminated bamboo flooring

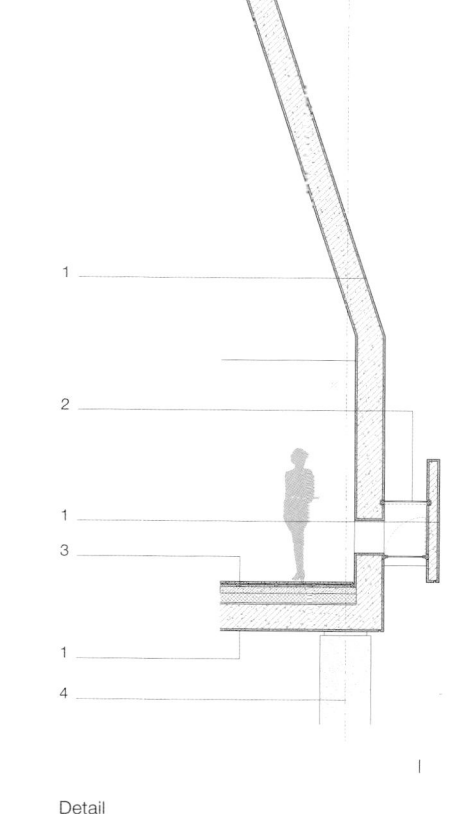

Detail

1. White stucco
2. 10 mm ultra-clear tempered glass
3. Laminated bamboo flooring
4. φ500 mm steel column with 50 mm concrete cover

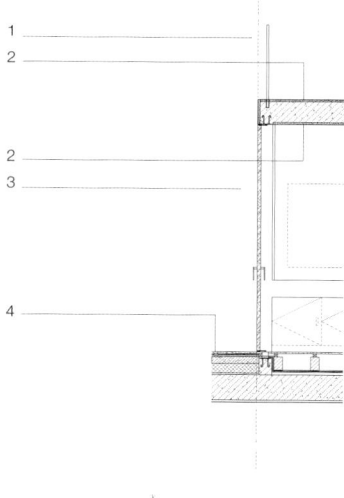

Detail

1. Steel railing 25 (w)x25 (d) mm, white fluorocarbon coated
2. White, textured spray paint
3. 40 mm laminated bamboo door
4. Laminated bamboo flooring
5. White quartz stone
6. Concrete wall with anticorrosive waterproof paint
7. Water feature

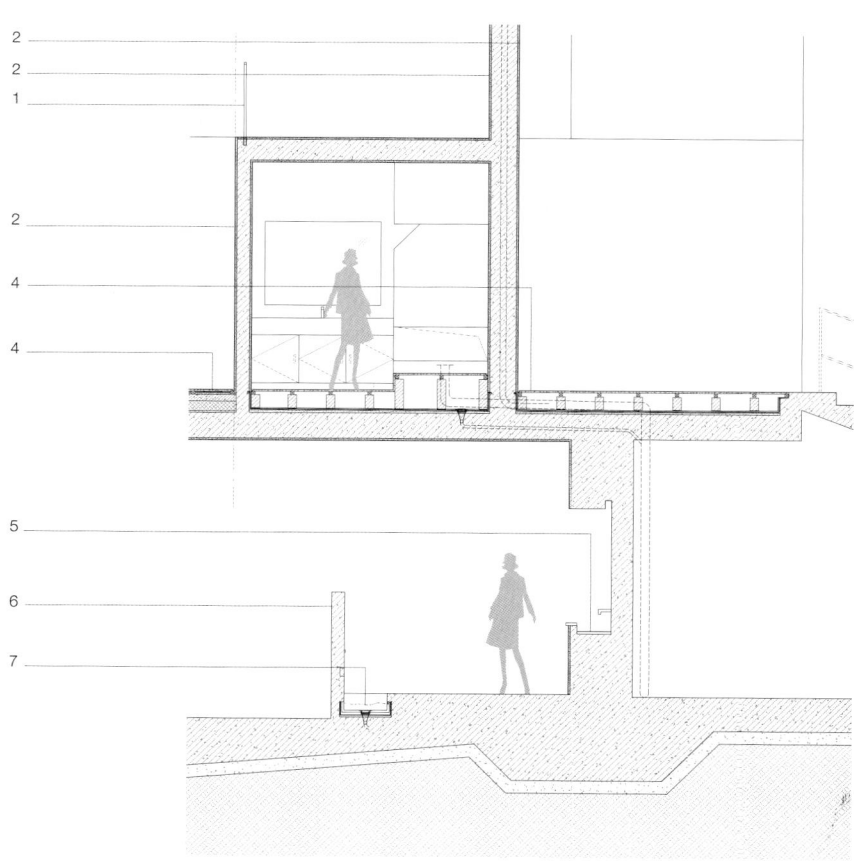

Summer 2025 45

Aranya Art Center

Lyndon Neri + Rossana Hu | Neri&Hu Design and Research Office

Location: Aranya Gold Coast Community, Beidaihe New District, Qinhuangdao, Hebei Province, China
Architect: Neri&Hu Design and Research Office
Principal architect: Lyndon Neri, Rossana Hu
Design team: Nellie Yang, Ellen Chen, Jerry Guo, Utsav Jain, Josh Murphy, Gianpaolo Taglietti, Zoe Gao, Susana Sanglas, Brian Lo, Lili Cheng
Gross floor area: 1,500 square meters
Design period: September 2016–May 2019
Photography: Pedro Pegenaute

Project aerial view

When developer Aranya asked Neri&Hu to design an art center inside their seaside resort community, Neri&Hu seized the opportunity, beginning the process by pondering on and questioning the notions of space regarding art versus communal space. The brief may have been straightforward, but Aranya, as a community, strongly emphasizes an oneness with nature—the spiritual nature of their lifestyle—and so the design scheme is as much about the internal courtyard and a communal space for the residents as it is about the exhibition being displayed in the center.

Drawing inspiration from the seasonal ocean waters nearby—azure and calm in the summers, splintered ice though winter—the building design attempts to encapsulate the natural wonder of water at its core. The scheme maximizes its outer footprint but carves out a pure conical geometry at the center with a stepped amphitheater at the base. The central void space can be reconfigured and used in many ways: a water feature when filled with water, but also a functional performance and gathering place when the water is drained. The exhibition galleries above benefit from the public space integration, which makes the project much more than just a place for display; it is also a place for sharing.

Within the thick mass of the building volume is a series of interlocking spaces that visitors can meander freely within, slowly ascending, enjoying a choreographed journey with views directed both inward and outward. Gallery spaces are about the enjoyment of art. This project is no different in that regard. A spiraling path leads you through all the spaces, urging you onward, overcome by a desire to see more. Starting at the bottom with the café, a multipurpose gallery and an outdoor amphitheater, the path guides you through five distinct galleries, culminating at the rooftop to proffer a 360-degree viewing experience of the activities below.

Aranya Art Center in the center of the Aranya community

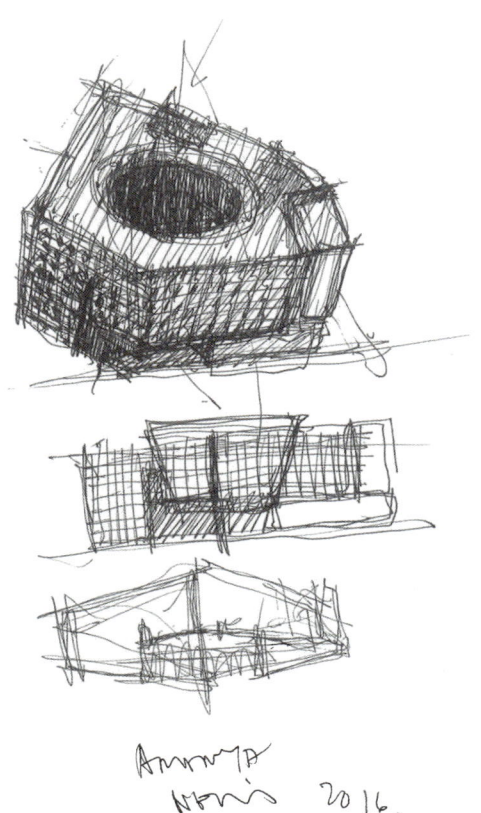

Neri&Hu's sketches

Entrance and elevations

Composed primarily of various textured concretes, with and without aggregate, the façade and materiality of the building is heavy in nature, like a solid rock sitting firmly in the shifting environment. Smooth surfaces reflect the changing skies, while the molded modular units pick up on the play of shadows throughout the day. Bronze elements act as accents on the heavy façade to catch light and draw attention to the entryway of each gallery. Custom lighting and details add a touch of intricacy to the otherwise modest palette. In the evening, open modules allow light to shine through, and the building becomes a jewel at the core of this seaside community.

Entrance

Atrium

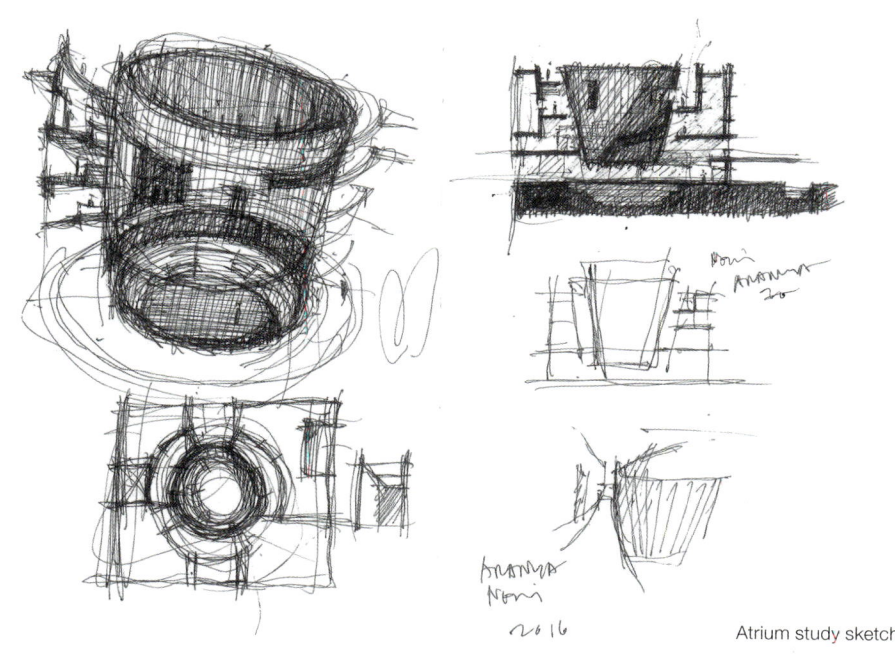

Atrium study sketches

Skylight

Atrium façade

View toward the sky

50   Architecture China

Corridor space

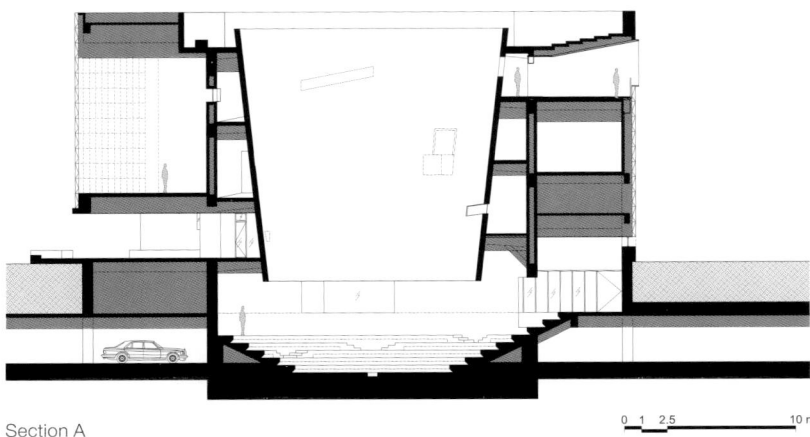

Section A

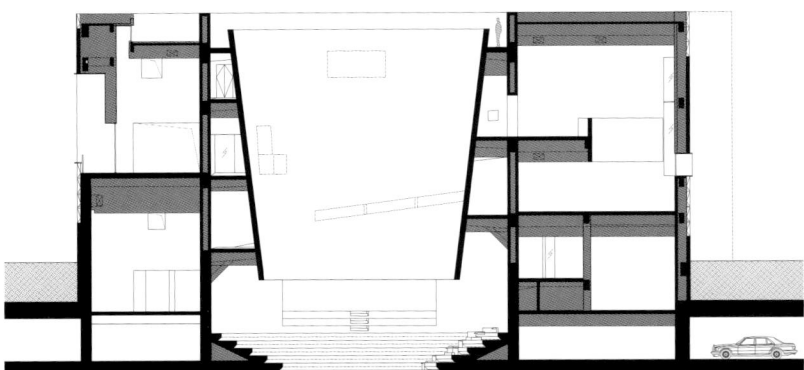

Section B

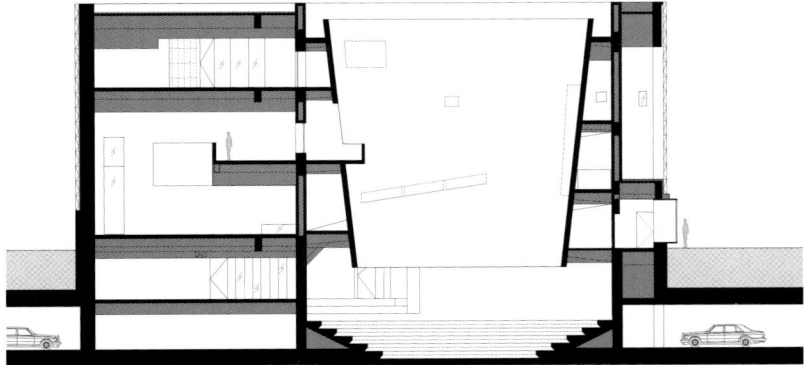

Section C

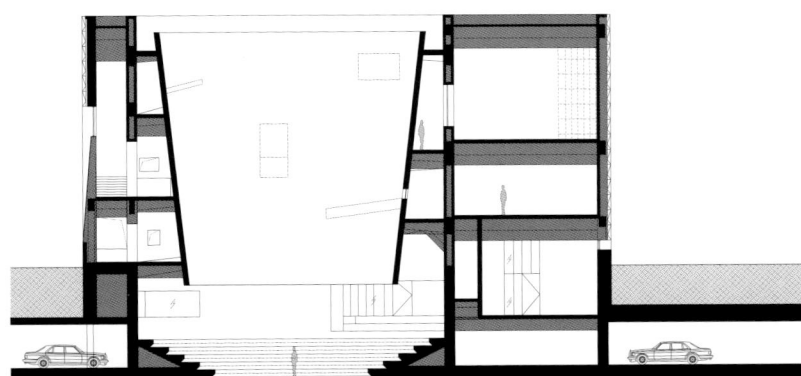

Section D

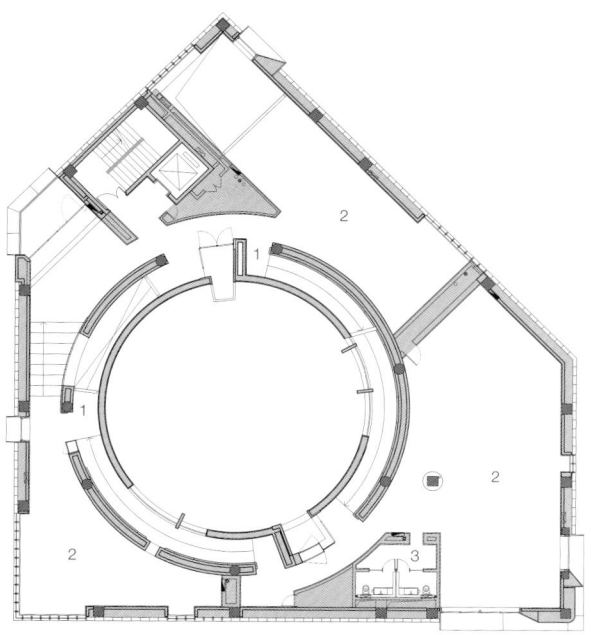

Second-floor plan

1. Circular ramp
2. Gallery
3. Restrooms

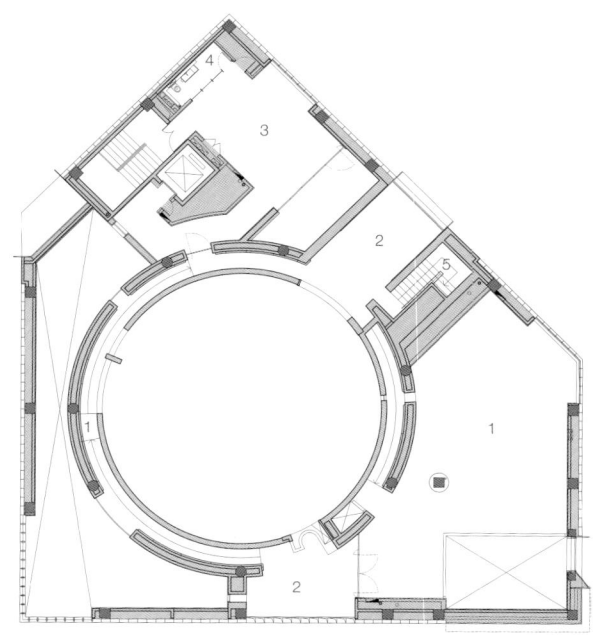

Third-floor plan

1. Circular ramp
2. Balcony
3. VIP room
4. Powder room
5. Stairs to rooftop

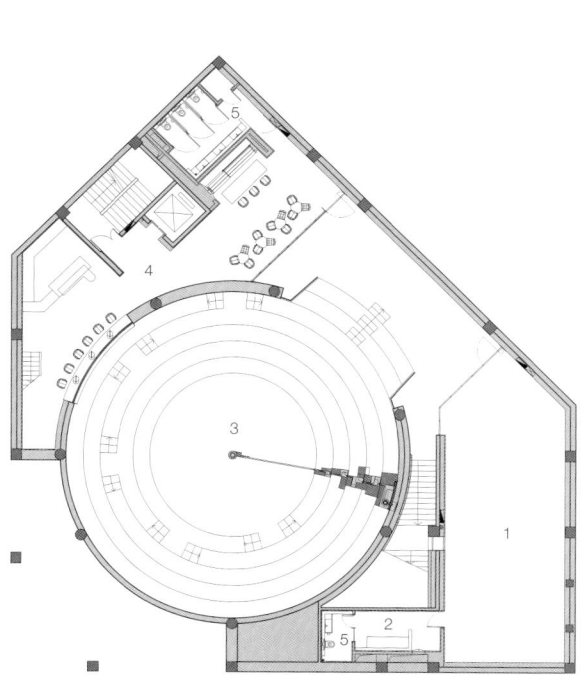

Basement plan

1. Multipurpose space
2. Changing room
3. Outdoor amphitheater
4. Café
5. Restrooms

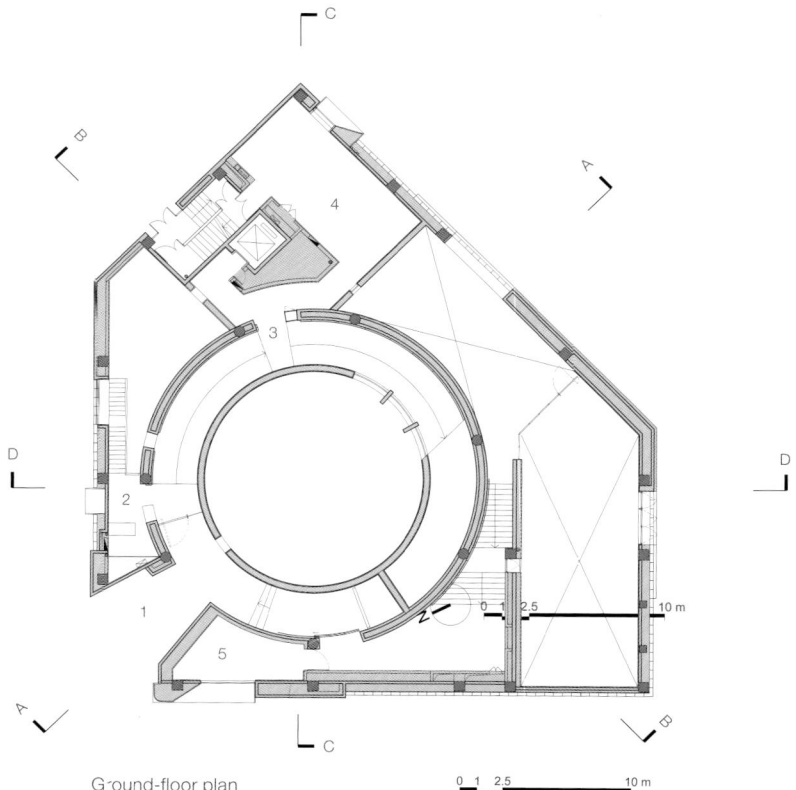

Ground-floor plan

1. Entrance
2. Foyer
3. Circular ramp
4. Gallery
5. Display vitrine

Summer 2025 53

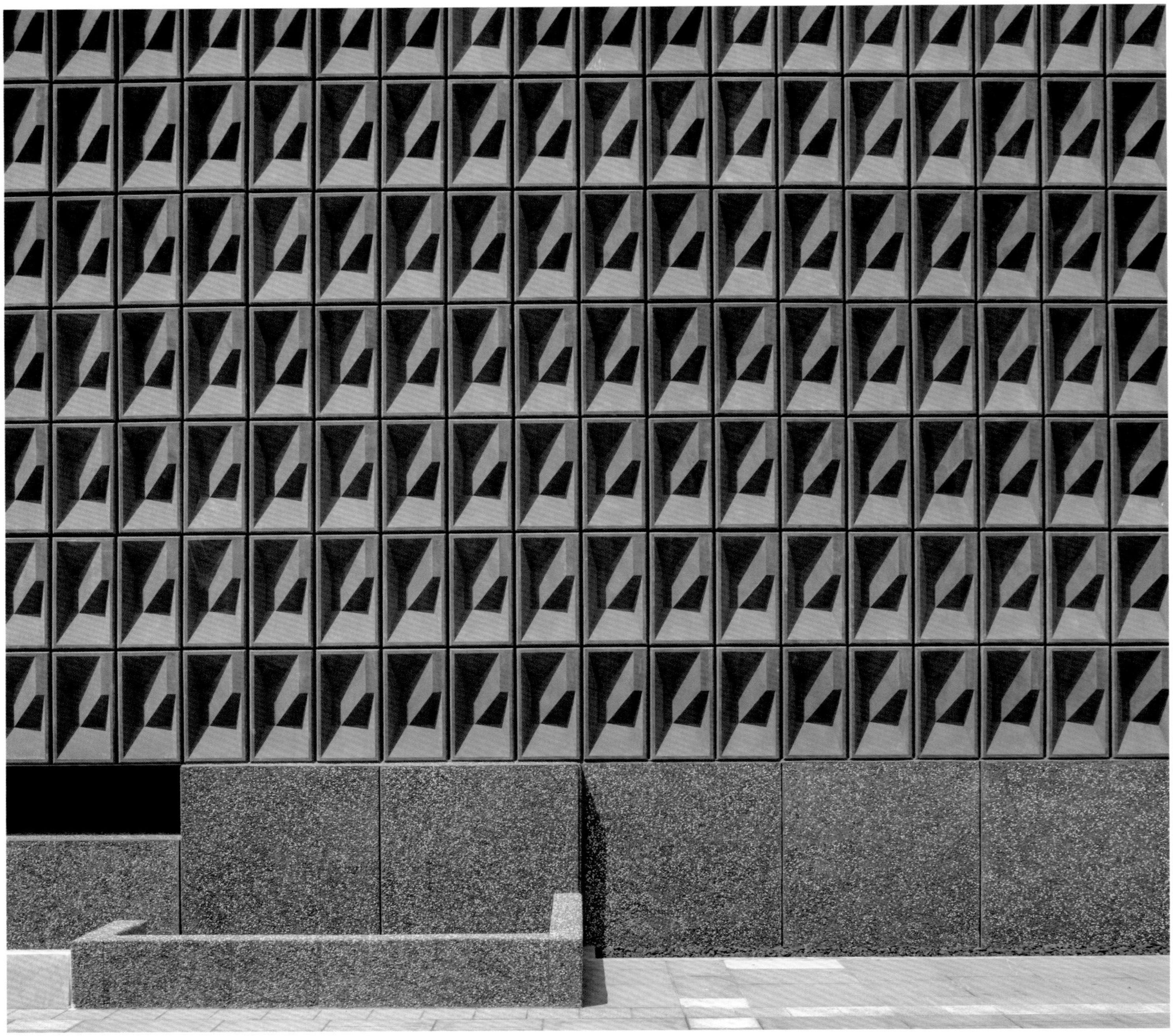

Close-up view of façade

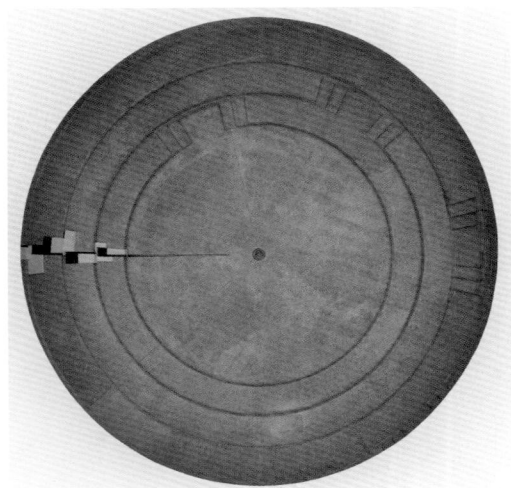

Aerial view of atrium

54 Architecture China

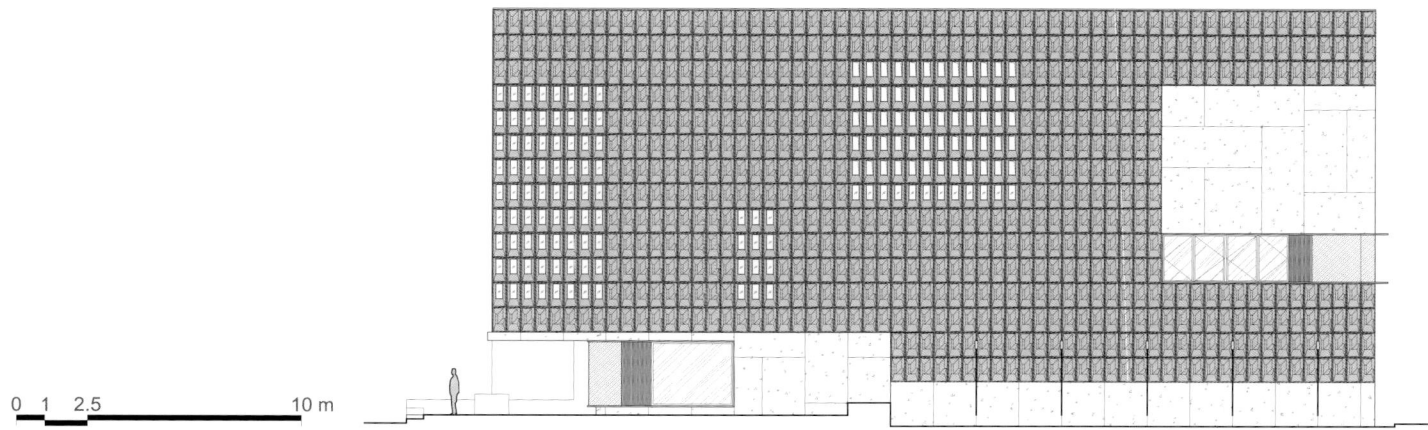

North–west elevation

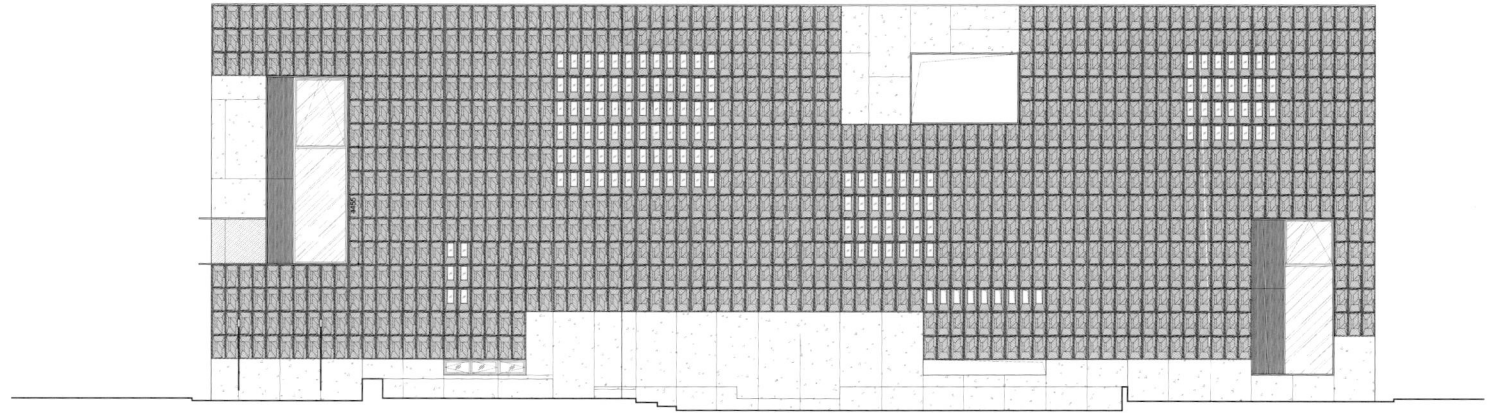

South elevation

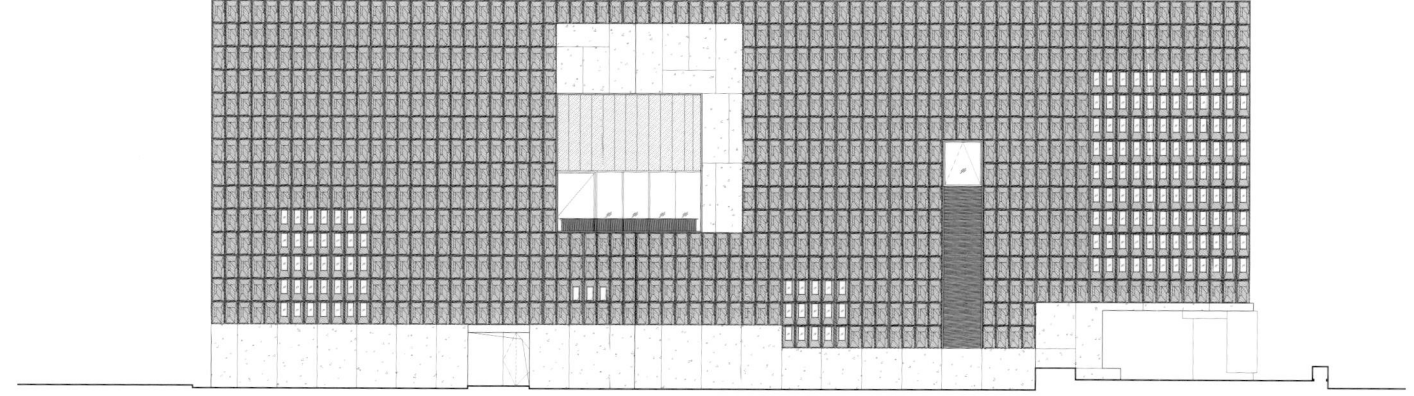

East elevation

UCCA Dune Art Museum

Li Hu + Huang Wenjing | OPEN Architecture

Location: Aranya Gold Coast Community, Beidaihe New District, Qinhuangdao, Hebei Province, China
Architect: OPEN Architecture
Principal architect: Li Hu, Huang Wenjing
Design team: Zhou Tingting (project architect), Wang Mengmeng, Hu Boji, Fang Kuanyin, Joshua Parker, Lu Di, Lin Bihong, Ye Qing, Steven Shi, Jia Han
Local design institute: CABR Technology Co., Ltd.
Lighting design: Tsinghua University X Studio + OPEN Architecture
Client: Aranya
Gross floor area: 930 square meters
Design period: 2015–2018
Photography: Wu Qingshan, Ni Nan, Zaiye Studio, UCCA Dune Art Museum

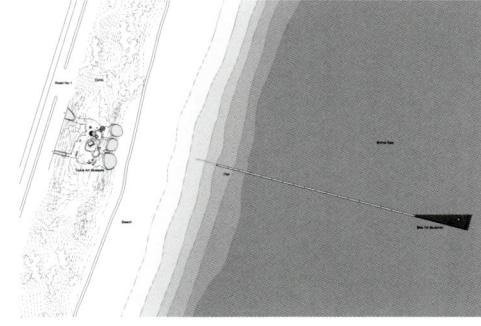

Site plan

On a quiet beach along the coast of northern China's Bohai Bay, the UCCA Dune Art Museum is carved into the sand, where it gently disappears.

Countless years of wind have pushed the beach's sand into a dune along the shore several meters high, stabilized by low-rising shrubs and other ground cover. The museum lies beneath this dune. Enveloped by sand, its interconnected, organically shaped spaces resemble caves—the primeval home of humans, with walls that were once a canvas for some of humanity's earliest works of art. Hidden between the sea and the sand, the design of the Dune Art Museum is simple, pure, and touching—a return to primal and timeless forms of space.

The decision to create the art museum underneath the dunes surrounding it was born out of both the architects' deep reverence for nature and their desire to protect the vulnerable dune ecosystem, formed by natural forces over thousands of years. Because of the museum, these sand dunes will be preserved instead of leveled to make space for ocean-view real estate developments, as has happened to many other dunes along the shore.

Looking through different openings framed by the building, museum-goers can observe the ever-changing expressions of the sky and sea throughout the day. A spiral staircase leads to a lookout on top of the sand dune, guiding curious audiences from the dark recesses below to the vast openness above. Underfoot, the museum emerges as a hidden shelter, intimate to the body and soul—a place to thoughtfully contemplate both nature and art.

Entrance © Zaiye Studio

UCCA Dune Art Museum facing Bohai Bay © Wu Qingshan

Gallery space featuring a skylight © Wu Qingshan

Lobby © Wu Qingshan

Café © Wu Qingshan

58 Architecture China

Spiral staircase leading toward the rooftop © Wu Qingshan

Looking down at the spiral staircase © Wu Qingshan

Looking down at the gallery space through the skylight © Ni Nan

UCCA Dune Art Museum at dusk © Wu Qingshan

Outdoor terrace to host exhibitions © Wu Qingshan

The complex three-dimensional geometry of the Dune Art Museum's concrete shell was shaped by hand by local workers in Qinhuangdao (some of whom were former shipbuilders), using formwork made from small strips of wood, and occasionally elastic materials when tighter curvatures were needed. The architects deliberately retained the irregular and imperfect texture left by the formwork, allowing traces of the building's manual construction to be felt and seen. In addition, the building's doors and windows, reception desk, bar counter, and bathroom sinks have all been custom-designed and made on-site. The eight tables in the café ave also been designed by the architects, each with a distinct shape matching that of the floor plans of the eight main gallery spaces.

The building's many skylights, each with a different orientation and size, provide carefully tempered natural lighting for the museum's spaces at all times of the year; its sand-covered roof greatly reduces the building's heat load; and a low-energy, zero-emission ground source heat pump system replaces traditional air conditioning.

Gallery space © Wu Qingshan

View from outdoor terrace toward the gallery space © Wu Qingshan

62 Architecture China

Gallery space © UCCA Dune Art Museum

Gallery space © UCCA Dune Art Museum

Summer 2025 63

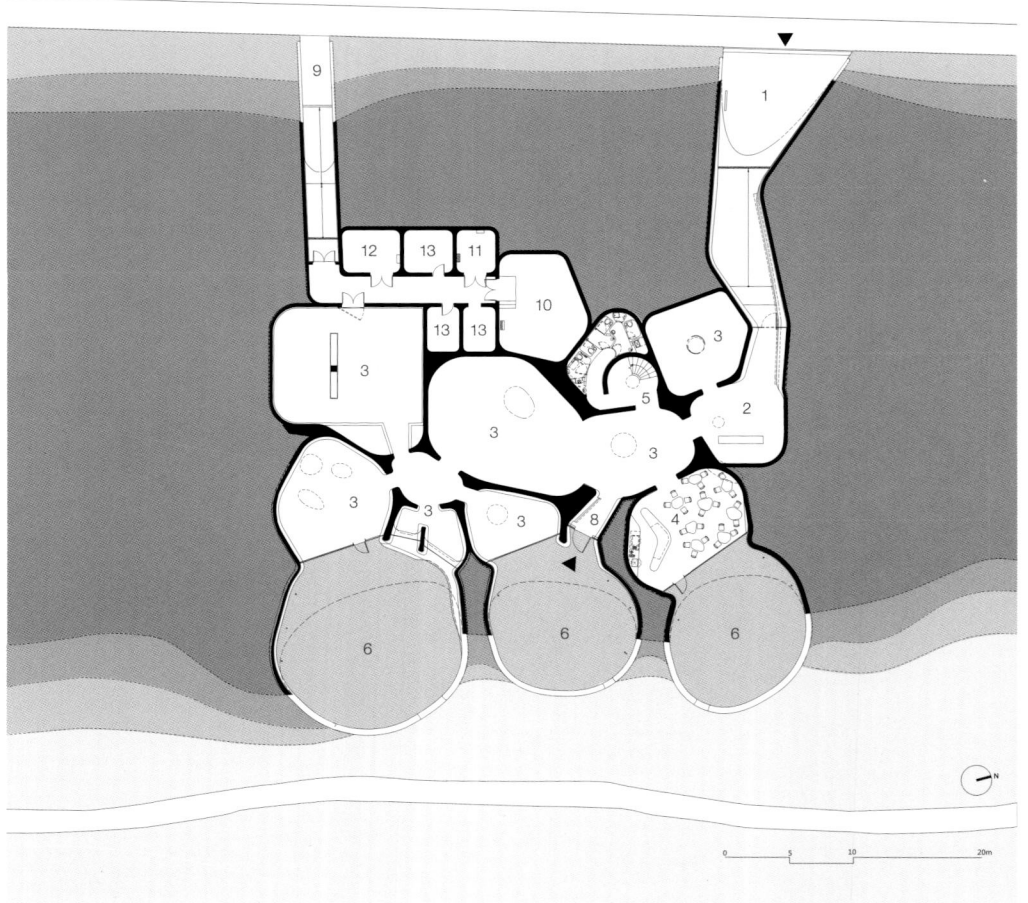

Ground-floor plan

1. Main entrance
2. Lobby
3. Gallery
4. Café
5. Stairs
6. Outdoor exhibition space
7. Toilet
8. Secondary entrance
9. Service entrance
10. Geothermal plant
11. Low-voltage room
12. Mechanics
13. Spare room

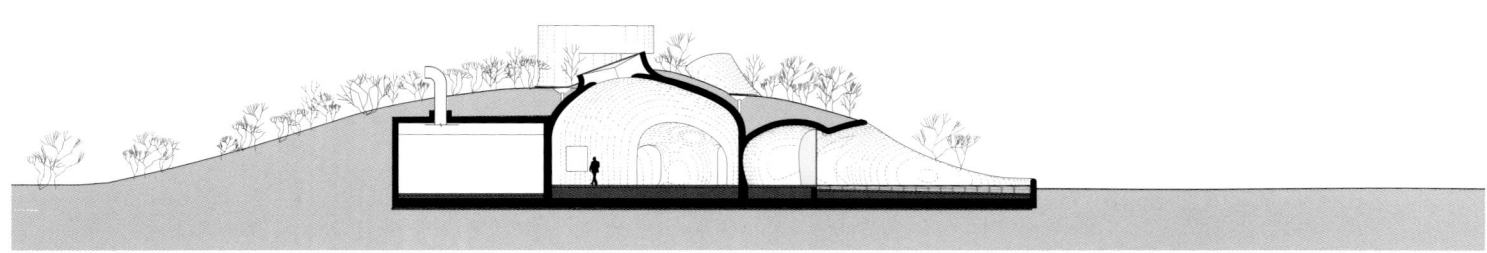

Section A

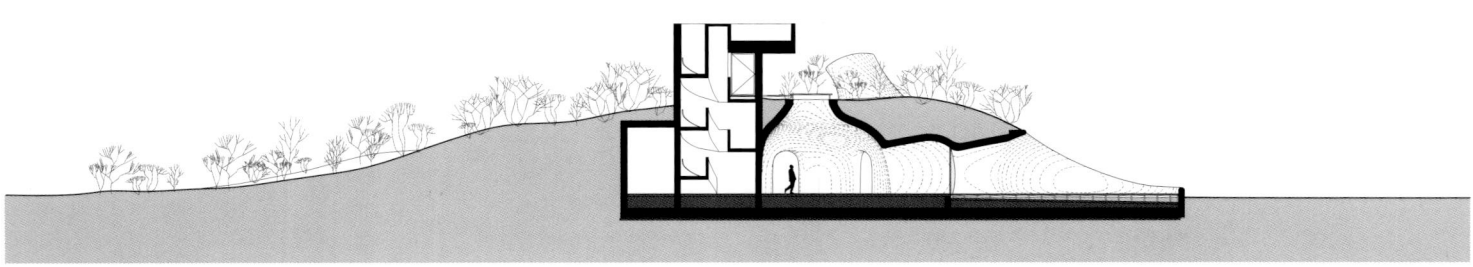

Section B

Section C

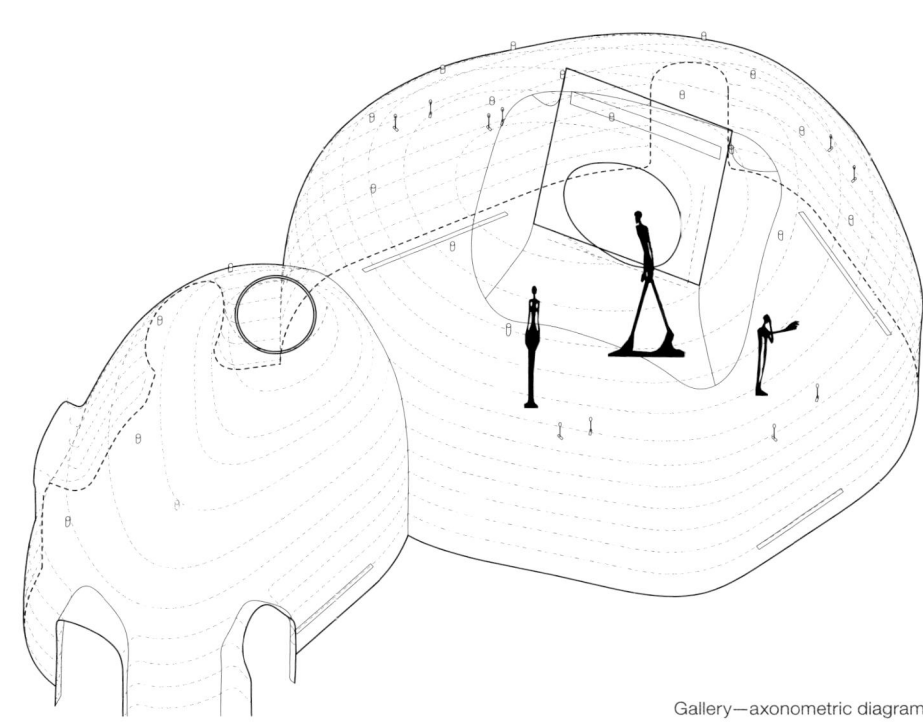

Gallery—axonometric diagram

Gallery space skylights
-direct sunlight throughout the year

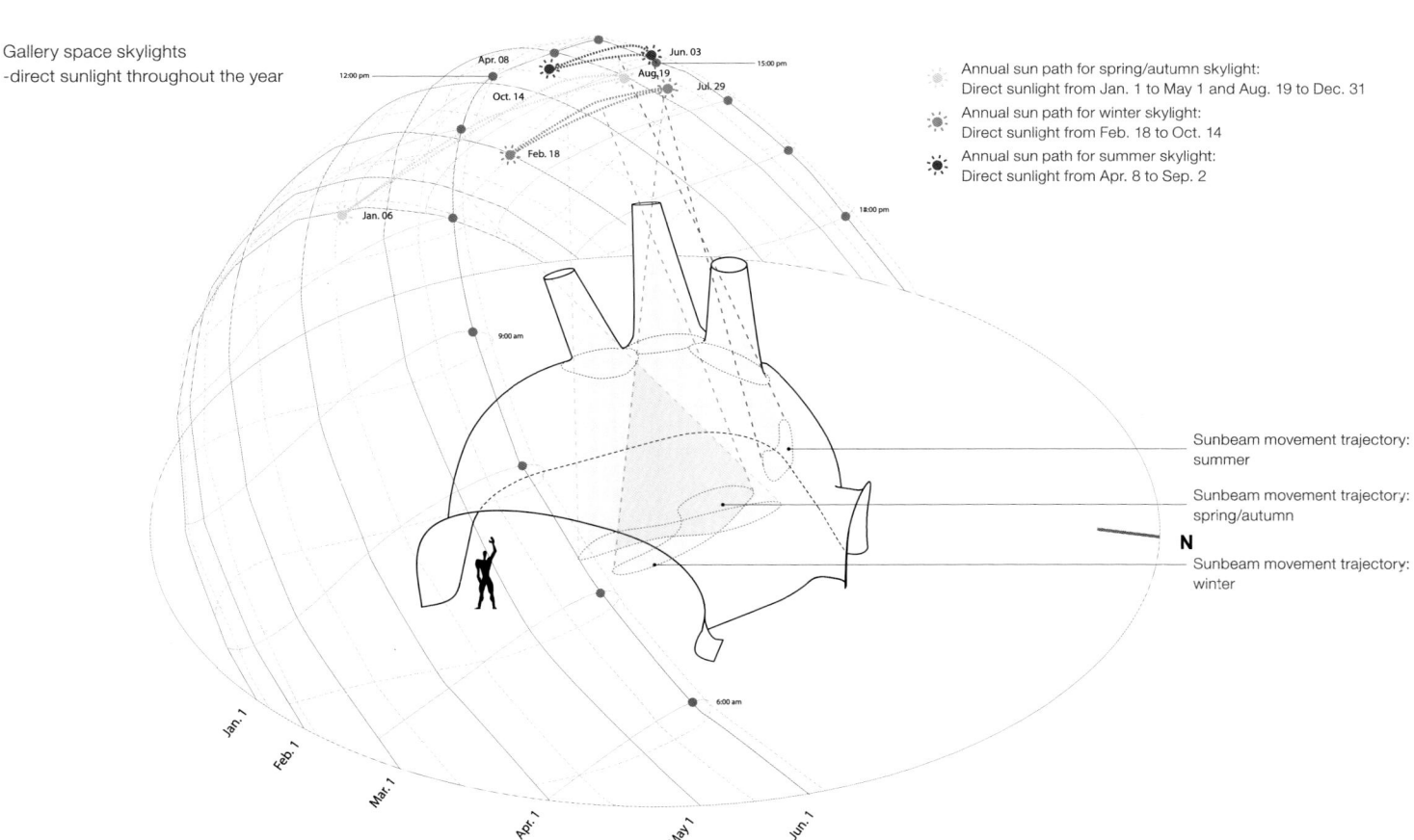

- Annual sun path for spring/autumn skylight:
  Direct sunlight from Jan. 1 to May 1 and Aug. 19 to Dec. 31
- Annual sun path for winter skylight:
  Direct sunlight from Feb. 18 to Oct. 14
- Annual sun path for summer skylight:
  Direct sunlight from Apr. 8 to Sep. 2

Sunbeam movement trajectory: summer

Sunbeam movement trajectory: spring/autumn

Sunbeam movement trajectory: winter

Game of Capitals: The Production of Influential Online Architecture

Zhao Xiaoxin
Postdoctoral research fellow, Nanjing University

Introduction

In the current new media era, existing forms of mass media have expanded and led to an information explosion. Many online social platforms and live stream platforms have also emerged, producing hundreds of thousands of online influencers in China, also referred to as *wanghong* (Cunningham et al., 2019). This phenomenon of the online influencer is not limited to people and has extended to architecture as well.

The Media—ranging from the print media of the past to today's online media—has played a significant role in shaping architectural culture and ideology (Wang, 2016). In current times, architecture and urban landscapes are robustly discussed and given wide attention through Instagram's "post" culture[1], as well as news reports. This has resulted in these structures and landscapes becoming influential online architecture (IOA) and influential online cities. However, at present in the Chinese context, there is limited literature that has examined the fundamentals of an IOA from an academic perspective (An and Fan 2019; Fan 2019; Yu 2018), and no academic literature on IOA has been found in the English context. This paper contributes toward narrowing this gap and aims to facilitate a better understanding of the emerging IOA phenomenon.

The primary focus of this paper asks how the IOA phenomenon emerged and what is its impact on the architecture field. Specifically, it reviews the IOA phenomenon from a rational perspective and strives to understand the types of IOA, as well as their characteristics, and the driving forces behind the coming to be of such influential online architecture. Based on the findings, the paper makes suggestions for future development in the architecture field.

The Emergence of the Online Influencer

Advertising is often used as a tool to help certain product aspects and information stand out and grab attention in order to drive sales and generate capital. Many advertisers take pains to constantly disseminate information across various media, repeating it often. This often got tied with celebrity branding and endorsements showcasing movie stars, sports icons, and even political and academic personalities and social elites. With the advancements of the Internet, however, more traditional media forms—print, TV, radio— are today giving way to self-media[2], causing a shift within media and capital markets from the star power of celebrity appeal to influencer appeal to promote a product, service, or even support a cause.

Online influencers refer to influencers refer to people who actively operate accounts on social media platforms, constantly uploading content to grab attention and increase their popularity. To some extent, an online influencer is similar to a DIY celebrity (Turner 2006) or microcelebrity (Senft 2008). Marwick (2013: 116–17, 121–23) argues that microcelebrities can be classified into two categories: ascribed and achieved. Ascribed microcelebrities usually emerge with a luxurious image and a higher status than their followers to attract their focus and attention, while achieved microcelebrities garner attention and trust with a grassroots image through intimate interaction with their online followers. Microcelebrities convert the online flow into money by attracting audiences' attention visually, but rely less on content production through videos or live streaming. In other words, online influencers have celebrity status not because they have demonstrable talents, abilities or contributions like traditional celebrities, but more because of their ability to attract attention on the Internet (Abidin 2018: 3). Once these online influencers gain a commendable following, usually hundreds of thousands of followers, they start to reel in lucrative endorsement deals and have their own trademark way of making money from their fame online.

From Online Influencer to IOA

With the explosion of social media, the online influencer phenomenon has extended to also include architecture, creating influential online architecture. The Chinese word *wanghong*, coined recently to refer to online influencers, has today inspired many enthusiastic discussions on *wanghong* architecture, referring to IOA in Chinese architectural media.

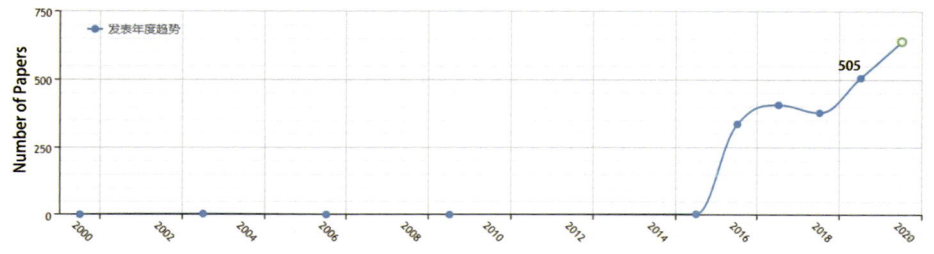

Figure 1: The number of academic papers with 'wanghong' in their title

In the China National Knowledge Infrastructure (CNKI) database, academic papers with wanghong in their title started to emerge in 2015 and increased dramatically from 2015 to 2019, representing the attention given to the online influencer phenomenon in the academic field (Figure 1). However, although there have been a significant number of academic discussions on wanghong within the fields of sociology, journalism, and communication, the academic discussion of wanghong in architecture and urban studies is still limited. As of October 2019, in the CNKI database, only two academic papers contained "wanghong architecture" their title and three contained "wanghong architecture" in their keywords.

Considering the term IOA, it is observed that "influential online" acts as the modifier of architecture. The true impact of "influential online" "influential" rather than "online."

Mass media has evolved since its early days to reign in online media today. Similar to mass media, architectural media has also developed through the times, from print architectural journals to the architectural bulletin board system to online social platforms. Print architectural journals and magazines have even established online social platforms as branches to expand their influence and attract more attention through sharing on the Internet.

The term "influential" denotes fame, reputation, popularity, and attention, which derive from diverse values. However, in architectural history, fame, reputation, popularity, and attention are derived primarily from a breakthrough in spatial design, form or structure, social significance, or the influence of that architecture on historical events. Today, the Internet makes people, products, and architecture popular in a convenient, hassle-free way, and IOA is an example of that.

Research Scope: Two Types of IOA

In this paper, IOA refers to buildings that have attracted broad attention from the public rather than any discussion within the architecture field. An IOA could either have been designed to catch attention or unintentionally does so, thereby classifying such influential architecture into two categories: after-end IOA and front-end IOA.

After-end IOA

After-end IOA refer to architecture that have gained popularity online unintentionally. Their online influence and popularity are not deliberately designed, but a result of events or unplanned factors that have been made trendy and popularized by ordinary users rather than stakeholders like designers or developers. For example, the Down Under the Manhattan Bridge Overpass (DUMBO) in New York became an influential district online because of the iconic scene in the movie *Once Upon a Time in America*. Similarly, because of the *Harry Potter* fantasy novel series and movies, the vicinity section of the fictitious platform 9¾ in London's King's Cross station gained fame online. In the same vein, the Blue Boat House, restored in the early 2000s, House on the shore of the Swan River in Perth, Western Australia, has become the hottest selfie spot and an Australian icon on Instagram with more than 20,000 hashtag posts. Just like how, La Muralla Roja, a postmodern apartment in Calpe, Spain, designed by Spanish architect Ricardo Bofill in 1968, became a popular spot posted widely on the Internet thanks to Monument Valley, a well-known smartphone game that copied the form of the apartment. These cases reflect that a place or space can also become a popular after-end IOA as an unexpected outcome resulting from movies, novels, social media, and even games.

Front-end IOA

Front-end IOA, the counterpart to after-end IOA, refer to architecture that has been designed with the intention of attracting public attention so that they become popular and generate capital. Buildings are often assigned as landmarks, providing profit for both internal and external stakeholders (Kirby and Kent 2010). Typically, right off the start of the design, architects and developers aim to catch the eye of the public and promote the project by self-branding, with the help of the media. A typical example is Vessel.

Vessel is an attractive landmark developed by real estate developer Stephen Ross in Hudson Yards as the "Eiffel Tower of New York." The building is an amazing staircase architecture that looks like a pine cone, designed by architect Thomas Heatherwick. It offers a variety of angles for photography with its landings and polished bronze surface, with proportions that adapt to well to the frame ratio of an Instagram post, so unsurprisingly, right after the building was completed in March 2019, classic photographs of the architecture were spread online, sparking vigorous discussions, which made the building an IOA. The developers also buit shopping malls, apartments, office towers, and hotels around the building, signifying that from the beginning, the architecture was defined as an eye-catching place that was expected to attract approximately two million visitors a year and bring inestimable income to the Hudson Yards district (Leading Architecture & Design, 2019), as is typical of a front-end IOA.

The paper restricts the discussion on front-end IOA, which is similar to what architecture professor, Fan (2019), referred to as auctorial IOA. He explained that the production of auctorial IOA is actively promoted by stakeholders through the propagation of collective anxiety and romantic or nostalgic consumption, together with the architecture.

Methodology

Research Framework: Bourdieu's Four Forms of Capitals

Like how online influencers came about for the purpose of making money by attracting public attention, an IOA comes to be so as a result of a series of human activities that are skewed to meet a particular need or have a certain aim, such as economic interests or profits. According to the German economist, sociologist, and political theorist, Marx (2007: 169–70), these economic interests and profits then turn into the capital. Therefore, capital theories can be applied to understand the needs and goals driving the IOA phenomenon. In the context of Marxist economics, capital usually refers to economic capital, including money and its means of production. However, capital is not restricted to an economic form.

French anthropologist and socialist Bourdieu (1986) innovatively explained his capital theory from a wider perspective and argued that capital takes other forms, too, like cultural and social capital, not just economic capital. His capital theory influenced Coleman (1988) and Putnam's (1993) social capital theories applied in sociology. However, Coleman and Putnam's capital theories mainly focused on the social dimension of capitals while IOA is a phenomenon that covers both economic, cultural, and social aspects. Therefore, linking back to Bourdieu's four forms of capital provides a key framework for analyzing the IOA phenomenon.

Bourdieu (1973, 1986) coined the term "cultural capital" and explained that cultural capital exists in three forms: The embodied state, that is, the understanding of culture that becomes part of personal knowledge and cultivation; the objectified state, that is, objects that store and represent culture, such as books, dictionaries, instruments and machines; and the institutionalized state, that is, certified cultural evidence that is recognized by society, such as educational qualifications. Cultural capital also has an embedded symbolic meaning. People obtain cultural capital to show their relationship to society and their "status" within it.

Bourdieu (1986) defined that social capital refers to "the aggregate of the actual or potential resources" that connect to the institutionalized membership of a group, which is determined by a durable social network with mutual acquaintance and recognition (Farr 2004). As a group or a nation, enhancing the cohesion of a society is a way to increase social capital to power development. Based on Bourdieu's viewpoint, Coleman (1988) argues that social capital is a type of resource that is embedded in the social network and Putnam (1993) argues that social capital is composed of social norm and trust. In Putman's argument, social capital designates national rather than personal wealth.

In addition to economic, cultural, and social capitals, Bourdieu also suggests the concept of symbolic capital, referring to the prestige and authority afforded by society. Symbolic capital is widely accepted in the economic, social and cultural capital distribution system that is recognized by society as a legitimate competence (Bourdieu and Wacquant 2013). Symbolic capital derives from the transformation of other forms of capital; it is evidence of the legitimacy of the other capitals and helps the flow of capitals.

Data Collection for Case Analysis

Applying Bourdieu's capital theory as a conceptual framework, the following sections will use case studies and logical argument, along with showing and analyzing relevant photos, statistical data, and comments from journals, books, news, and social platforms to examine how the IOA phenomenon emerged.

This paper will examine IOA case studies in China for two reasons. First, as there is no existing term that has been commonly used to refer to IOA in the English context, the IOA cases in this paper have been collected from online media by searching for "*wanghong* architecture," which is the commonly used term referring to IOA in the Chinese context. Second, as a Chinese citizen, the author has a better understanding of the Chinese economic, cultural, social, and political context to analyze the IOA phenomenon. However, taking into account the architecture of Vessel, the paper admits that the IOA phenomenon occurs globally; this will be discussed later.

The paper argues that IOA are not designed by but controlled by capitals, and is produced by intentionally manipulating the media. In order to reveal the relationship between IOA and different forms of capitals, selected cases will be categorized based on Bourdieu's four forms of capital. Specifically, as a tool for capital transformation, an IOA normally seeks capitals in four ways, namely as visual spectacles, or through class division, national identity, and social recognition.

Game of Capitals: The Production of IOA

IOA: Visual Spectacles and Economic Capital

IOA offer visual spectacles with the intention to attract public attention. These visual spectacles can be classified into two categories: miracle IOA and freak IOA.

Miracle IOA refer to visually attractive architecture with a fashionable form that usually obtains appreciation from the public, such as Vessel. The recent rapid urbanization in China has seen the building of a few miracle IOA. For example, a pyramid-shaped combined residential and commercial apartment complex, also used as an office building in Kunshan, China, became an Internet sensation on social media due to its amazing architecture and appearance. Huang (2018) reported that because of its amazing look, this apartment block had sold out with 90 percent occupancy, which was a higher tenancy ratio than in the other buildings around it. This photogenic building has attracted hundreds of visitors, who post their photos online and contribute to the tourism economy in Kunshan.

Freak IOA attract people's attention with vulgar forms through rough imitation. From the perspective of forms, freak IOA are to some extent similar to what architects Robert Venturi and Denise Scott Brown define as a "duck" rather than a "decorated shed" (Venturi et al. 1977: 88). The "duck" refers to a building-come-sculpture architecture, which expresses its function as a symbol, while the "decorated shed" refers to an ornament/embellishment that is applied independently, pointing to the function of the building (Venturi et al. 1977: 87–88). As the key figures in postmodernism, Venturi and Brown critiqued modern international-style buildings as ugly and boring "duck" buildings that pretend to be extraordinary, and support the "decorated shed" as a functional building with meaningful symbols that enrich architectural diversity. A huge Chinese softshell turtle and a huge crab stand as prominent "ducks" in China today, their zoomorphic architecture aimed at attracting the public eye.

Although opinions differ when it comes to defining the aesthetic distinction between miracle IOA and freak IOA, there is no denying that both these IOA offer visual spectacles which draw people's attention. Among the three principles of good architecture asserted by Vitrivius (durability, utility, and beauty), only beauty can be read directly through an image , attracting attention and delighting spirits. In the fast-reading era of the Internet, more attention means more money, so it is inevitable that architecture demands an attractive image. As an image can spread rapidly because of online social media, IOAs are designed with visual spectacles to attract people's attention quickly to generate economic capital.

IOA: *Xiaozi* Class Division and Cultural Capital

Aesthetics and taste are important indexes of cultural capital and cultural division that are influenced by and reflect people's social class (Le Roux et al. 2008). In the voice of the media, IOA often represent good taste and aesthetics as 小资 (*xiaozi*). Xiaozi is short for 小资产阶级 (*xiao zichan jieji* petty bourgeoisie), defined and critiqued by the China Communist Party as the corrupt, weak-minded, idealistic and nihilistic social class. However, after the 1990s, *xiaozi* became a commendatory word in China that was used to refer to the social class that had become rich and who respected culture and spiritual enjoyment, boasting excellent taste, an eye for aesthetics, and elegant behavior. Their *xiaozi* identity is reflected in their lifestyle and taste. Within this context, in China, the *xiaozi* class creates a symbol of distinction against their cultural capital and social class through their aesthetic inclinations, tastes, and consumptions (Bourdieu 2010: 12), such as watching cult films, consuming more premium brands like Starbucks or Häagen-Dazs, and eating at Michelin-starred restaurants in China. These behaviors, as symbols of distinction, show the way to obtain cultural capital and represent a higher tier of social class (Gartman 1991). The everyday person then imitates these aesthetics, tastes and consumption behavior to obtain their cultural capital, as if they, too, have become a higher social class.

Although symbols of distinction represent cultural capital and social class, they are not static and are always changing, determined and propagated by the upper class. Compared to obtaining personal knowledge, cultivation, and educational qualifications, accessing symbols of distinction is easier, and so ordinary people strive to obtain the symbol of distinction as cultural capital. However, when obtaining symbols of distinction becomes effortless, the *xiaozi* class will change their tastes and construct new symbols of distinction to distinguish themselves as elite, so as retain their social class (Gartman 1991). New luxury products or services will be selected by the upper class as the new symbols of distinction and the media will be paid to propagate this distinction to attract the common person's consumption by advertising the constantly changing symbols of distinction as new cultural capital. Through this cycle, the everyday person will obtain the so-called cultural capital and the media and the upper class will obtain economic and symbolic capital.

When considered against this perspective, IOA take on the role of a new symbol of distinction. Their attractive architectural image bring economic capital to the developers; they also bring cultural capital to ordinary consumers and visitors. In addition to to captivating imagery, sometimes moving poetic words are added to extend romanticized sentiments that boost the appeal of IOA. One well-known example is the article "The Loneliest Library in China" accompanied by attractive photographs. Creative, compelling verses and interesting photos crafted the library into an Instagram-worthy subject in no time at all (Yitiao 2015).

The sea is dyed a dark colour; the sunshine passes through the cloud and disappears intermittently. The library stands alone on an open beach, like a simple and hard stone that has existed for decades. The surface of the concrete walls, without decoration, record the construction process, with the trace of timber moulds that make you feel the warm touch of the timber.

"The sunlight illuminates the meditation room through a narrow gap, reflecting the passage of time. Through the window of the meditation room, the panorama of the reading room jumps into view. The beams of light enter the space from various directions and play a symphony with warm and cold tones" (Yitiao 2015). This well-worded description offers a picturesque and intoxicating tableau the as if retaining the impressions of the timber molds on the concrete walls becomes an excellent aesthetic in architectural language; and if there was no dark meditation room with a glorious light beam, the design seems to lose its elegance. This description also reflects the architect's strategy to use the loneliness characteristic of the building to attract public attention to tailor it into an IOA.

As soon as the library was completed, it hit the headlines in Chinese social media, and media reports contributed to a misleading impression that reading or visiting the library was elegant because of its "loneliness." Here, loneliness becomes a symbol of distinction that reflects superior aesthetics and taste, bringing cultural capital to the ordinary people visiting the library. Ironically, after it became the loneliest library in China, "nearly 2,000 people visited one Saturday afternoon to experience noise instead of loneliness" (Williams 2015).

It is a reversal of the proper order when taking a photo of the library and posting it on Instagram because of its isolation seems to have become the first priority for a library; whether or not it is used as a library has become unimportant. A question was posted on the online question and answer platform 知乎 (Zhihu) in China: What is your experience of visiting the loneliest library in Qinhuangdao? Zhihu users responded that "there [are] limited books in the library" "no one visits there for reading;" and that "most of them are visitors but not readers who just need some nice photos to post on their social platforms" (Zhihu 2015).

The library, an auxiliary project for the Aranya tourism and real estate , used promotional material adapted to the posting culture and flaunted the *xiaozi* lifestyle to the public. Following in the footsteps of the "upper class," the everyday person also wished to display his/her distinctive taste by posting photos with the library to obtain cultural capital, which has made the library an IOA.

IOA: National Identity and Social Capital

As the aggregate of the actual or potential resources that connect to the institutionalized membership of a group, social capital exists not only in personal social networks but also in groups (Putnam 1993). Communities, companies, institutions, and even a nation will strengthen connections and enhance the cohesion of the society between members to increase the social capital to power development.

National architecture, built for national events that represent the national identity, often become IOA because they illustrate the national identity and culture, enhancing the sense of pride and social cohesion among citizens. Therefore, national IOA are intentionally designed as tools to increase a nation's social capital, such as the Effiel Tower in Paris.

To meet the requirement of strengthening national social capital, the official media and mass media contribute to broadcasting and reporting every stage of national architecture, from site selection to the design scenario until completion, so that the national architecture is officially created as an IOA and is known by almost every citizen. National IOA in China include, for example, the Olympic National Stadium and National Aquatics Center in Beijing; the China pavilion at Expo 2010 in Shanghai; the National Centre for the Performing Arts; and the China Central Television (CCTV) building. National architecture also feature catchy nicknames that contribute to making them IOA. Some national IOA have official nicknames, such as *Bird's Nest* (the Olympic National Stadium), *Water Cube* (the National Aquatics Center), and *Oriental Crown* (the China pavilion at Expo 2010); other national architecture are given colloquial nicknames, such as *the boiled egg* (the National Centre for the Performing Arts) and *the big underpants* (the CCTV building). All in all, the demand for national social capital is the primary driving force that makes this type of architecture IOA.

Let us take the CCTV building as an example. There was some controversy that as a well-renowned architecture firm, The Office for Metropolitan Architecture (OMA) disobeyed architectural ethics to design such a weird and extravagant building. Ole Scheeren, the director of the CCTV building project in OMA, defended the architect's design during a speech at Columbia University with two main points: Firstly, the design was the CCTV's choice, not OMA's choice; and secondly, he insisted that constructing such extravagant architecture was customary to represent China's national identity during its urbanization years. He cited the "ten national architectures" in Beijing that were built in 1958 to 1959 as an example to illustrate that only China could turn a historic city into a modern city by constructing so much extravagant architecture as its national identity in such a short time, proving that design on a grand scale and in extravagant forms is reasonable (Zhu 2014: 332–35).

As Beck (1998: 115) said, "Architecture is politics with bricks and mortar." Architecture plays a role as a medium that broadcasts the history, culture, and identity of a nation, as well as the national ideology. In European countries, architecture has been used in the discourse as an "expression of post-national identities within and beyond nation-states" and imperial powers (Delanty and Jones 2002). Similarly, in building a national identity and increasing social capital in China, architecture has been a significant tool since the 1910s. Chinese architects tried to establish a Chinese architectural style in the 1930s, and when the People's Republic of China was founded in the 1950s, the socialist ideology influenced and utilized national architecture as a medium to represent its national identity to increase social capital, such as the ten national architectures in Beijing (Wang and Wang 2014). The construction of the ten national architectures cannot be viewed separately from the historical background of the 1950s, when China had just ended its civil war. The new Communist Party government needed these ten national architectures to act as the face of the country to build national identity and increase the national social capital for the construction of a new China.

From this perspective, the state government's need for social capital promotes national architecture as IOA.

IOA: Social Recognition and Symbolic Capital

In the production of IOA, reviews and comments on the IOA are strongly related to the architect's social recognition and determine the architect's symbolic capital. As a subject, the boundary of architecture is ambiguous and vague, so that both professionals and the public have the opportunity to evaluate architecture projects. The voices of professionals in the field and the public have become entwined in modern-day's online era to influence subsequent design works (Fan 2019). Furthermore, the timeliness and the relative freedom of online comments and discussions contribute to a stronger interactive evaluation model for reviewing architectural projects (Li and Zhi 2014). Thus, to encourage acceptance of the public, architects sometimes will break from architectural and design autonomy and take as guide the public voice, probably influenced by the motto "be famous as early as you can" the online influencer community. Architects usually find three shortcuts to fame—public persona, media promotion, and awards—to increase personal symbolic capital and become star architects or influential online architects (Yu 2018).

On the angle of public persona, architects are becoming involved in the world of showbiz, participating in television shows such as 梦想改造家 (*mengxiang gaizaojia*/renovation for the dream home) or 漂亮的房子(*piaoliang de fangzi*/the beautiful house) to reveal their private design process to increase the attractiveness of the architect's image. At times, they are also featured in advertisements, sometimes with other celebrities, to increase their discoverability and heighten their social recognition through media exposure, and obtain symbolic capital.

Online social media plays a significant role in producing IOA and influential online architects. Qualified influential online architects require more than design skills; they also need excellent writing skills and the ability to promote projects with the help of the media. Architect and critic, Yu (2018), took on the Mulan Weichang Visitor Centre project on *piaoliang de fangzi* to illustrate his argument. From the time the show broadcast the project in December 2017 up until today, the Mulan Weichang Visitor Centre has been the object of more than four million Google searches in Chinese and 179,000 searches in English. The media took every effort to promote the project with clickbait, using phrases like "The Mongolian yurt designed by Daniel Wu's[3] group wins the architecture award" and "The lonely Mongolian yurt in China." Yu (2018) collected and counted the titles of relevant online articles pertaining to the project from December 21 to 31, 2017 and explained that the high-frequency keywords were Daniel Wu, Mongolian yurt, architecture award, loneliness, and the phrase "the most beautiful." These eye-catching words used by the media contributed to the project gaining IOA status. He added (2018) that good-looking, talent and super renovation were overused words in IOA.

Architects are also applying for various national and international awards such as the Red Dot Award and the iF Design Award, to elevate their fame, reputation, and qualifications to obtain symbolic capital. To win an award, many architects fall into a trap of social value or political correctness. Upon examining the winners and nominees for the Pritzker Architectural Award (PAA) in the recent years, one picks up that this award focuses on the social value of the design. For example, the 2013 and 2014 PAA winners, Japanese architects Toyo Ito and Shigeru Ban; the 2016 PAA winner, Chilean architect Alejandro Aravena; and the 2018 PAA winner, Indian architect Balkrishna Doshi all espouse architectural practices with positive social influences and values, such as post-disaster reconstruction or designing for low-income groups. Patrik Schumacher, director at Zaha Hadid Architects, says that:

> *The role of the architect is now "to serve greater social and humanitarian needs," and the new laureate is hailed for "tackling the global housing crisis" and for his concern for the underprivileged. Architecture loses its specific societal task and responsibility, architectural innovation is replaced by the demonstration of noble intentions and the discipline's criteria of success and excellence dissolve in the vague do-good-feel-good pursuit of "social justice"* (Commercial Interior Design 2016).

This paper argues that advocating social justice is not a fault, but the fake social justice that caters to any award selection standard is definitely a misconception. This misconception reflects in the inconsistency between the initial slogan and final result of the design. For example, the revitalization of Wencun village is designed from a somewhat "fake social justice" perspective that advocating rural revitalization should respect traditional construction techniques as the intangible cultural heritage and meet the modern needs of local villagers. However, this project did not use traditional construction techniques and the villagers' attitude toward the project was not as positive as reported by the mass media (Dong, 2015, p. 94). The villagers were dissatisfied with the project until the village become an influential online village, whereupon visitors were attracted and many of the houses in the village were turned into bed-and-breakfast hotels, bringing economic profits. Obviously, this phenomenon went against the architect's original purpose and was not in line with his claims (Zhao and Greenop, 2019). These cases illustrate architects make efforts to obtain symbolic capital by promoting their architectural projects as IOA.

IOA is Promoted by Combined Capitals

Using well-known architectural examples, this paper has elaborated on four forms of capital that separately create IOA; however, it does not mean each IOA is promoted by only a single type of capital. For instance, in addition to the cultural capital sought by tourists, the "lonely library" also encourages economic capital as an auxiliary project for the Aranya real estate project. Dong Gong, the architect, had also submitted the "lonely library" project to many journal and magazines and awards to enhance his symbolic capital by being known as a star architect. Meaning to say, some IOA may have primary and secondary capital promotors rather than just one.

IOAs promoted by multiple capitals are not restricted to China; they are, and have been, making tracks globally, too, such as the Sydney Opera House (SOH) for example. The SOH is a unique example because it gained popularity in an era where only print and broadcast media existed. Other examples include the Guggenheim Museum Bilbao and Louvre.

As a predecessor IOA, the SOH was also intentionally designed as a landmark of Sydney and promoted by cultural, social, and symbolic capitals. As cultural capital—a new opera house was advocated in the 1950s to offer music and performances to the Australian people (Kerr 2003: 13). As it was to be marked a national opera house, the Australian government announced an international competition and attracted public attention globally. As social capital—Muratovski (2012: 198) notes: "Architecture is in a sense a promotional medium and an identity definer. It is a medium that promotes social relationships and individual enterprises, and can be used as a symbol of territorial identity." In this sense, the SOH has been designed as a national iconic architecture that creates social capital by giving Australians a "sense of attachment that communities have with this place" (Freeman 2018: 44). As symbolic capital—Jørn Utzon, an unknown 38-year-old architect in 1957, became the winner of an international competition to design Sydney's national opera house, relying on his innovative but controversial design. He was later chosen as the 2003 Laureate of the Pritzker Architecture Prize for the SOH.

Although the SOH was not initially designed for the tourism economy, with the contribution of online social media, the SOH has truly become an IOA today, with more than 860,000 posts on Instagram with the hashtag #sydneyoperahouse. Statistics show that the SOH attracts thousands of tourists to Sydney every year and it was estimated to contribute AU$640.1 million to dollars spent in Sydney in 2012 to 2013, through encouraging overnight stays and visitor spending (Scerri et al. 2019). The balance between capitals and design makes the SOH a successful example of an IOA.

Discussion

Zukin (2009: 15) argues that when analyzing urban development we should consider the political economy and sociocultural factors, including the power of economic capital, the state, the cultural power of the media, and consumer tastes. Among these factors, the cultural power of the media and consumer tastes offer people more second-hand rather than first-hand experience—for example, people want to see the ratings and reviews of local food, shopping spots, services, and entertainment first by using apps such as Yelp[4] before making their decision, which influences their direct urban experience. And when an increasing number of people give ratings and reviews based on their experience of an architecture or urban space in journals, magazines, blogs, and other social media, the second-hand experience is perpetuated and spreads. From this perspective, IOA rely on the cultural power of the media and consumer tastes through disseminating a second-hand architectural experience.

In this sense, an IOA is a product of the combined fields of architecture and communication, and is becoming a reproducible architecture that adapts to capital flow. That means, the mass media contributes to broadcasting an image of the IOA as the vehicle for capital flow and transformation through "value-add through propagation" (An and Fan 2019). This propagation may be manipulated by stakeholders for seeking different capitals (Fan 2019). The case studies reviewed have shown this: real estate developers invest in IOA to obtain economic capital, tourists visit IOA for cultural capital, governments promote IOA projects for social capital, and architects design IOA for their symbolic capital.

On a positive note, IOA promote the spread of excellent architectural experiences, encourage and attract more people to visit, and create an interactive public urban space. However, on the flip side, not all IOA will be constantly attractive and retain popularity, especially front-end IOA that are designed with the intention of attracting public attention and capital. We should be wary that because of the driving force of capitals, even inferior designs could become IOA if promoted by the mass media, to pave a quick route to capital and profit. At present, the media is willing to promote architects through puffery, and architects enjoy becoming idols because of the capital and profit gain, which negatively affects the design field. An and Fan (2019) critique that "form follows finance" and that architecture design has been forced by the financial market. Therefore, this paper argues that in the process of IOA production, the overemphasis on capitals may cause "bad money" to drive out "good money"[5] in the design field, meaning that an inferior design may drive out a good design.

Conclusion

This paper offers a novel perspective in reviewing architecture with media. It has distinguished two categories of IOA: after-end IOA and front-end IOA, and used case studies to illustrate that the IOA phenomenon is promoted by capitals with the help of the media. As front-end IOA is designed as a tool for capital transformation, the overemphasis on obtaining capitals in the production of IOA may erode architectural design.

To avoid IOA eroding the design aspect, architectural academic and management departments should establish a democratic architectural critiquing and post-occupancy evaluation (POE) system, especially in China. An anonymous Zhihu user, who was an architectural journal editor in China explained: "Critical articles criticizing architecture are usually rejected by our chief editor because it runs contrary to the theme of a Socialist Harmonious Society"[6] (Zhihu 2018).

Architectural criticism contributes to the theoretical development of architecture and urban design. In China, architecture journals and media normally introduce architectural practices from a positive perspective, such as architecture historians and theorists writing papers to flatter these practices with obscure theories. Real and profound architectural critiques of architectural practices and theories are limited (Li and Zhi 2014). Compared to architectural practices, architectural critiques secure a quicker reaction to the current issues in the built environment and society with a shorter period and a stronger time-effectiveness. During the process of critiquing, valuable ideas and philosophy will emerge to guide future architectural and urban development. Simultaneously, architectural critiques consider the influence of the building not only on the value of architecture itself, but also on people's lives in widely covered dimensions, such as community interaction and health. Thus, to prove the objectivity, criticism, and comprehensiveness of its voice, the media should keep a proper distance from stakeholders in the architecture field to protect its autonomy and independence. However, in China, there are many more discussions on the topic of architectural critique than there are on architecture critics themselves in China (Jin, 2009) and, ironically, non-professional online users discuss and criticize the image and the social influence of IOA more enthusiastically.

POE is the process of "systematically comparing actual building performance with explicitly stated performance criteria: (Preiser 1995: 19). It is also a tool that concludes the current issue of the design and makes suggestions to improve future work. POE is an after-end mode that offers an objective evaluation of architecture by experts and people rather than the front-end IOA that propagates pre-supposed interpretations. Therefore, POE plays a significant role in establishing positive values and criteria for future design as it at the same time attempts to resist inferior IOA.

In the end, architecture, media, and capital are increasingly connected. Online media not only contributes to producing IOA for capitals, it also offers platforms for architectural criticism and POE to guide future architectural and urban design. The paper suggests using the IOA mode properly to rationalize and balance architectural and urban design with capitals.

The author(s) discloses receipt of the following financial support for the research, authorship, and/or publication of this article. This work was supported by the China Scholarship Council [201506190144].

Notes

1. The posting culture has existed for decades and even centuries. Before the popularization of the camera, people carved their names on tree trunks or walls in scenic spots to represent them having visited these places. Now, with the wide use of smartphones with digital cameras, the posting culture has been relocated to online social platforms, such as Instagram.

2. Traditional media refers to newspapers, magazines, posters, radio, television, and exhibitions. Self-media refers to independently operated social media accounts on platforms such as Instagram, Twitter, and TikTok, usually run by individual users.

3. Daniel Wu is an actor from Hong Kong, China who studied architecture at the University of Oregon. He participated in the TV show *piaoliang de fangzi* and designed the Mulan Weichang Visitor Center with architect Zhang Hai'ao. Known for his good looks, Daniel Wu's participation in this program attracts many female fans who watch this television show.

4. Yelp is a business directory service forum, accessed through its website and the mobile app, which publishes crowd-sourced reviews about businesses.

5. Also called Gresham's law; this means if there are two types of money with similar face value in circulation, the money that has more commodity value (the value of the metal from which it is made) will gradually disappear from circulation.

6. The phrase "Socialist Harmonious Society" was coined by former China president Hu Jintao to create societal harmony as a response to the increasing social issues caused by injustice and inequality.

References

1. Abidin, C. Internet Celebrity: Understanding Fame Online. Leeds: Emerald Group Publishing, 2018. https://doi.org/10.1108/9781787560765.
2. An, K. and W. Fan. "The Transformation of Architectural Design with Reality: The Case of the Eight Tenths Garden and Related Designs." New Architecture, (5) 2019: 92–96.
3. Beck, U. "The Open City: Architecture and Reflexive Modernity." Democracy Without Enemies. Cambridge: Polity Press, 1998, 115–121.
4. Bourdieu, P. "Cultural Reproduction and Social Reproduction." Knowledge, Education and Cultural Change. Edited by Richard Brown. London: Tavistock, 1973, 71–112.
5. Bourdieu, P. "The Forms of Capital." Handbook of Theory and Research for the Sociology of Education. Edited by J. G. Richardson. New York: Greenwood Press, 1986, 241–258.
6. Bourdieu, P. Distinction: A Social Critique of the Judgement of Taste. London: Taylor & Francis Group, 2010.
7. Bourdieu, P., and L. Wacquant. "Symbolic Capital and Social Classes." Journal of Classical Sociology vol. 13 (2) 2013: 292–302. https://doi.org/10.1177/1468795X12468736.
8. Coleman, J.S. "Social Capital in the Creation of Human Capital." American Journal of Sociology 94, 1988: s95–s120.
9. Cunningham, Stuart, David Craig, and Junyi Lv. "China's Livestreaming Industry: Platforms, Politics, and Precarity." International Journal of Cultural Studies 22 (6) 2019: 719–736. https://doi.org/10.1177/1367877919834942.
10. Delanty, G., and P. R. Jones. "European identity and architecture." European Journal of Social Theory 5 (4) 2002: 453–466. https://doi.org/10.1177/136843102760514009.
11. Dong, Yiping. "Wencun Village, China, by Wang Shu and Lu Wenyu's Amateur Architecture Studio." The Architectural Review, November 17, 2015, 92–103.
12. Fan, W. "Four Phenomena of Chinese Architectural Media in the Internet Age." Time + Architecture 2, 2019: 41–47.
13. Farr, J. "Social Capital: A Conceptual History." Political Theory 32 (1) 2004: 6–33. https://doi.org/10.1177/0090591703254978.
14. Freeman, C. G. Participatory Culture and the Social Value of an Architectural Icon: Sydney Opera House. New York: Routledge, 2018.
15. Gartman, D. "Culture as Class Symbolization or Mass Reification? A Critique of Bourdieu's Distinction." American Journal of Sociology 97 (2) 1991: 421–447.
16. Huang, Ying. "Pyramid-like Complex an Internet Sensation." Global Times. September 6, 2018. http://www.globaltimes.cn/content/1118553.shtml.
17. "Patrik Schumacher Says 'the Pritzker Prize Has Mutated into a Prize for Humanitarian Work'". Industry Insight. Commercial Interior Design. January 20, 2016. Accessed March 4, 2019. https://www.commercialinteriordesign.com/thoughts/patrik-schumacher-says-the-pritzker-prize-has-mutatedinto-a-prize-for-humanitarian-work.
18. Jin, Q. "What is the Function of Architectural Critiques?" Architecture Journal 5, 2009: 72–73.
19. Kerr, J. S. Sydney Opera House: A Plan for the Conservation of the Sydney Opera House and its Site. Sydney: Sydney Opera House Trust, 2003. https://doi.org/10.1080/13556207.2005.10784952.
20. Kirby, A. E., and A. M. Kent. "Architecture as Brand: Store Design and Brand Identity." Journal of Product and Brand Management 19 (6) 2010: 432–439. https://doi.org/10.1108/10610421011085749.
21. Le Roux, B., H. Rouanet, M. Savage, and A. Warde. "Class and Cultural Division in the UK." Sociology 42 (6) 2008: 1049–1071. https://doi.org/10.1177/0038038508096933.
22. Li, L., and W. Zhi. "Landscape of Communication of Contemporary Chinese Architectural Criticism in the Mass Media Since 1980." Time + Architecture 2, 2014: 40–43.
23. Marwick, A. Status Update: Celebrity, Publicity, and Branding in the Social Media Age. New Haven: Yale University Press, 2013.
24. Marx, K., Capital: A Critique of Political Economy. New York: COSIMO Publications, 2007.
25. Preiser, W. F. E. "Post-Occupancy Evaluation: How to Make Buildings Work Better." Facilities 13 (11) 1995: 19–28. https://doi.org/10.1108/02632779510097787.
26. Putnam, R. "The Prosperous Community: Social Capital and Public Life." The American Prospect 13 (4) 1993: 35–42.
27. Scerri, M., D. Edwards, and C. Foley. "Design, Architecture and the Value to Tourism." Tourism Economics 25 (5) 2019: 695–710. https://doi.org/10.1177/1354816618802107.
28. Senft, Theresa M. Camgirls: Celebrity and Community in the Age of Social Networks. New York: Peter Lang, 2008.
29. Turner, Graeme. "The Mass Production of Celebrity." International Journal of Cultural Studies 9 (2) 2006: 153–165. https://doi.org/10.1177/1367877906064028.
30. Venturi, R., D. S. Brown, and S. Izenour. Learning from Las Vegas: The Forgotten Symbolism of Architectural Form. Cambridge: MIT Press, 1977.
31. Vessel, 2019. Lead. Archit. Des. 12. [15] Vessel. Leading Architecture & Design, 2019(3): 12.
32. Wang, H. "Tracing the 100-year Development of the Chinese Architecture Print Media." World Architecture 1, 2016: 54–63.
33. Wang, K., and Y. Wang. "Conceptual Mapping and Four Genealogies: Evolving Discourses in Chinese Architectural Media of the 20th Century." Time + Architecture 6, 2014: 28–33.
34. Williams, Austin. "This is No Chinese Copycat." The Architectural Review 238 (1425) 2015: 56–65.
35. Yitiao. "The Loneliest Library in China." Archcollege, 2015. http://www.archcollege.com/archcollege/2015/5/14637.html.
36. Yu, Y. "Architecture as Media Blockbuster." Time + Architecture 4, 2018: 110–119.
37. Zhao, X., and Kelly Greenop. "From 'Neo-Vernacular' to 'Semi-Vernacular': A Case Study of Vernacular Architecture Representation and Adaptation in Rural Chinese Village Revitalization." International Journal of Heritage Studies 25 (11), 2019: 1128–1147. https://doi.org/10.1080/13527258.2019.1570544.
38. Zhihu. 2015. "What is Your experience of Visiting 'the Loneliest Library' in Qinghuangdao?" Accessed March 4, 2019. https://www.zhihu.com/question/30302242.
39. Zhihu. 2018. "Do Papers in Architectural Journals Have Direct Critiques?" Accessed March 4, 2019. https://www.zhihu.com/question/23712274/answer/356197924.
40. Zhu, T. Liang Sicheng and His Times. Nanning: Guangxi Normal University Press, 2014.
41. Zukin, S. Naked City: The Death and Life of Authentic Urban Places. Oxford: Oxford University Press, 2009.

Tiantai No. 2 Primary School

Ruan Hao + Zhan Yuan | LYCS Architecture

Location: Tiantai, Zhejiang Province, China
Architect: LYCS Architecture
Principal architect: Ruan Hao, Zhan Yuan
Design team: Gary He, Jin Shanliang, Chen Lina
Local design institute: Zhejiang University Urban Research & Design Institute
Gross floor area: 1,010 square meters
Design period: 2012
Construction period: 2013–2014
Photography: Yu Xu, Su Shengliang

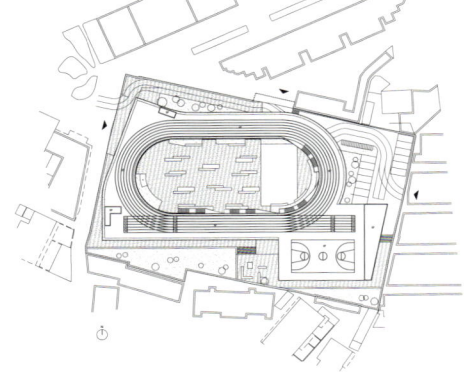

Site plan

The Tiantai No. 2 Primary School project strives to establish a unique design that will serve as a model elementary school that provides a beautiful environment for the cultivation of knowledge, culture, physical fitness, art, and ethics. The project effectively solves the problem of land shortage in the old city. The 200-meter running track was projected onto the roof level, instead of placing it the ground as is traditionally done, freeing-up an additional 3,000-square-meters of usable area on the ground as well as the oval shape of the school building, creating a sense of inwardness and security for the students as well as allowing for a lightness in the space instead of cramped surroundings. Lifting the running track also allows for a total project height of four floors instead of five as originally required, creating a more harmonious relationship between the new school and the surrounding urban context. In order to create more available green courtyard spaces, the building is twisted about 15 degrees, creating smaller pockets of space between the wall and the exterior envelope.

The rooftop track has three layers of guardrail to guarantee the safety of students. The exterior layer is a 1.8-meter-high tempered glass wall; the middle layer is a 50-centimeter-wide green belt, and the interior layer is a 1.2-meter-high stainless-steel guardrail. For the issue of noise, the spring cushions are put every 50-by-50 centimeters under the plastic track, thus reducing further kinetic noise by way of the double-layer structure.

Students running on the track © Yu Xu

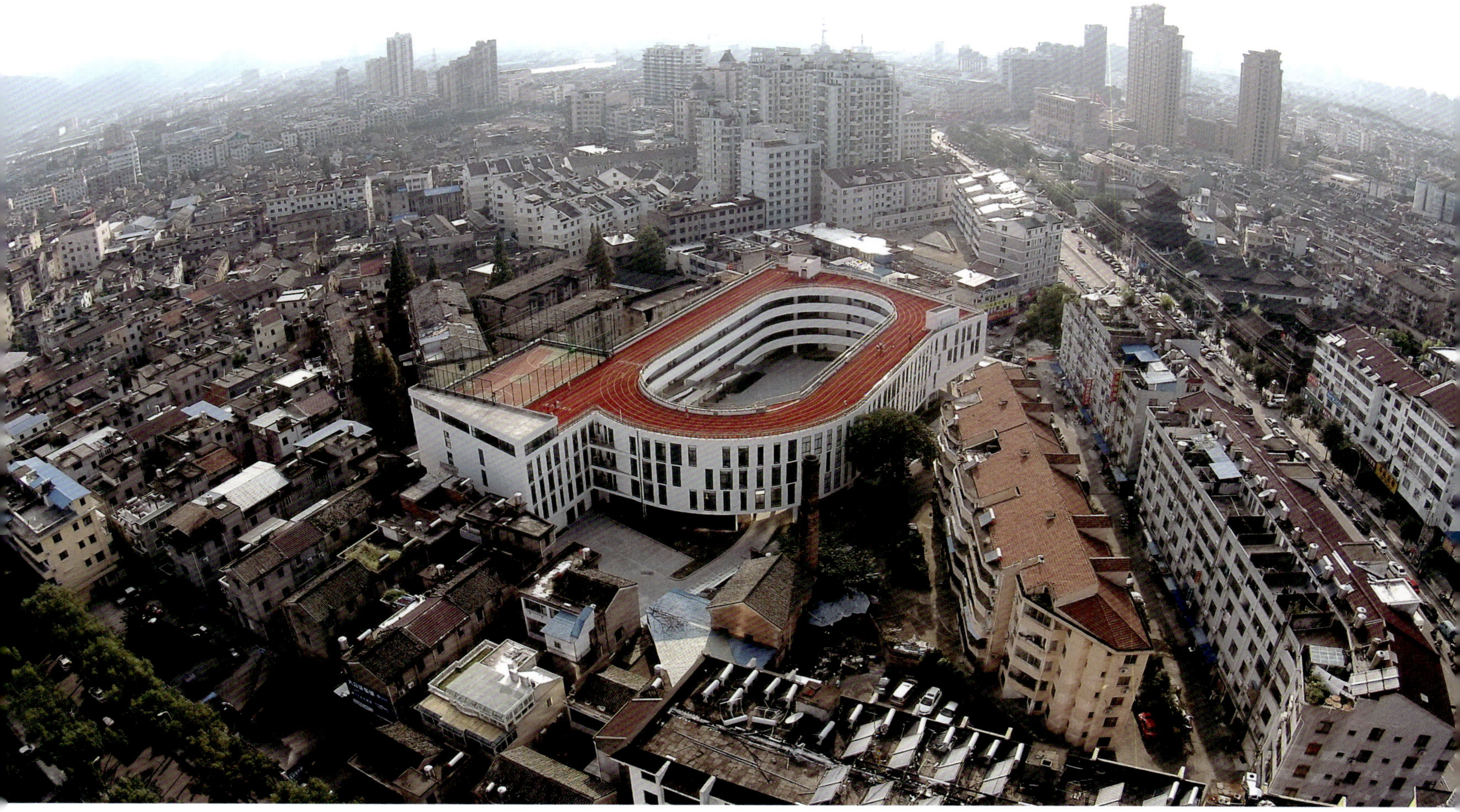

Aerial view © Su Shengliang

The Tiantai No. 2 Primary School in a high-density area © Su Shengliang

Students exercising on the field © Su Shengliang

Staircase leading toward the rooftop © Su Shengliang

Staircase and the courtyard © Su Shengliang

Elevation with a grid pattern © Su Shengliang

View from corridor toward the courtyard © Su Shengliang

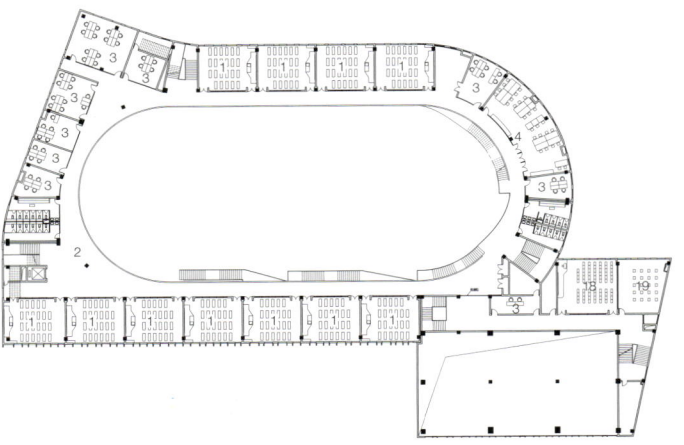

Fourth-floor plan

1. Classroom
2. Corridor
3. Office
4. Laboratory

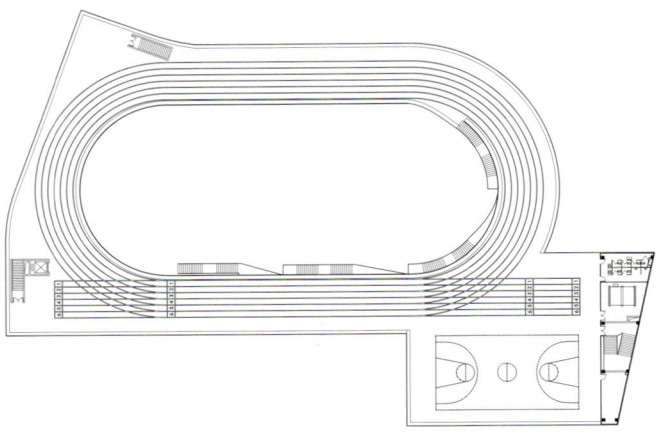

Rooftop plan

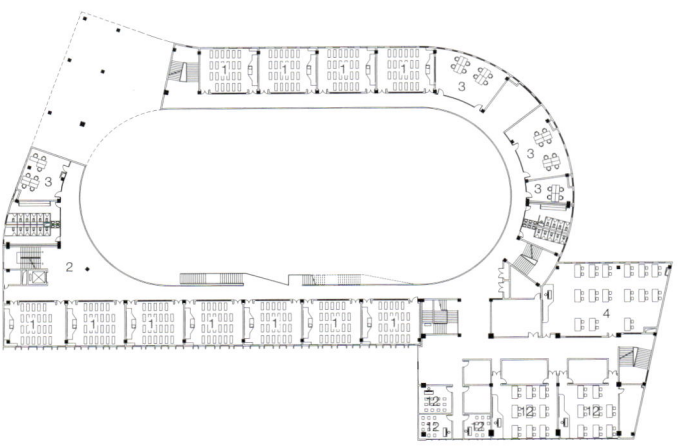

Second-floor plan

1. Classroom
2. Corridor
3. Office
4. Laboratory

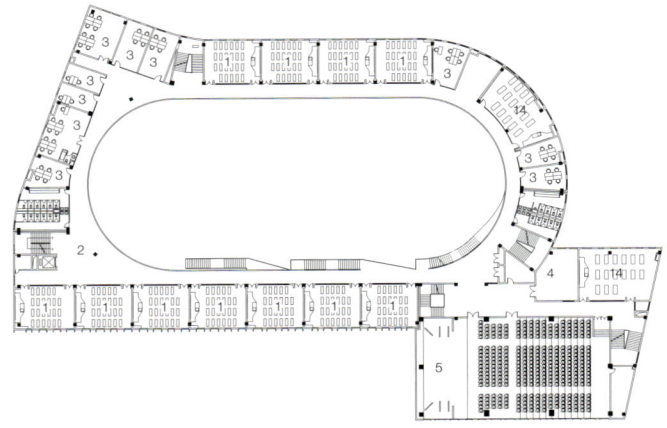

Third-floor plan

1. Classroom 4. Laboratory
2. Corridor   5. Auditorium
3. Office

Model

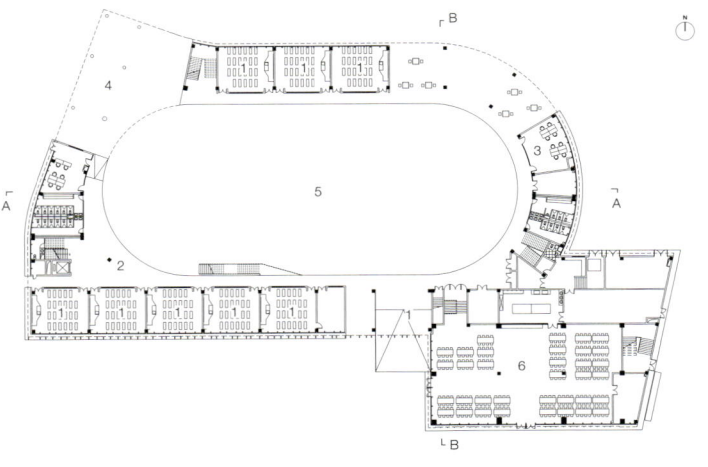

First-floor plan

1. Classroom 4. Entrance
2. Corridor   5. Playground
3. Office   6. Canteen

78 Architecture China

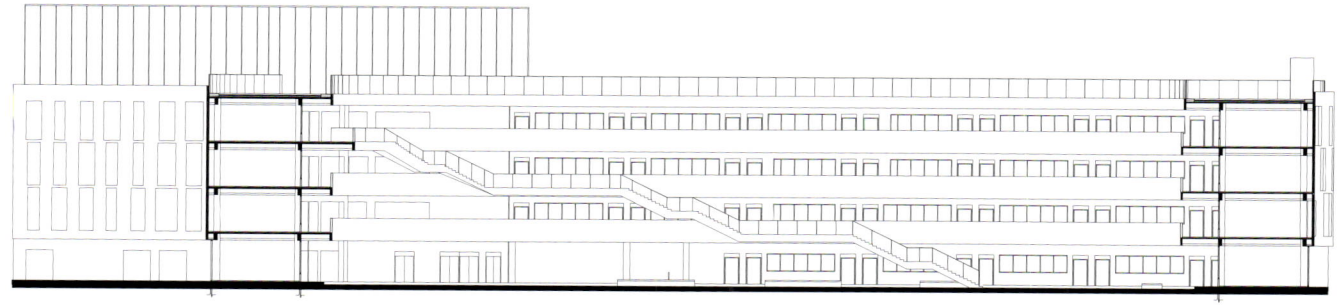

Section A

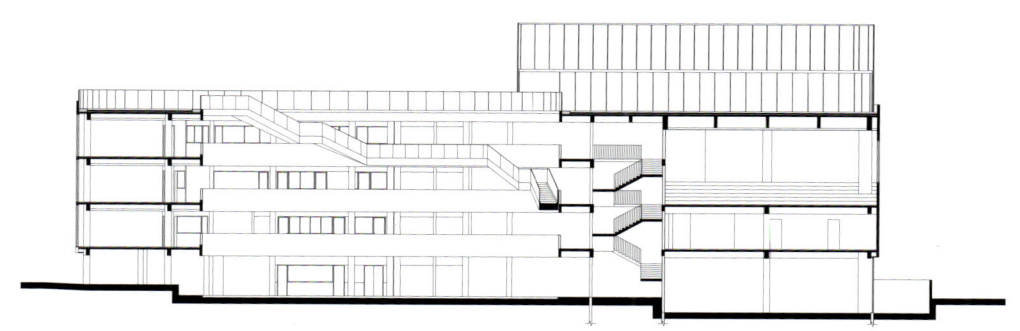

Section B

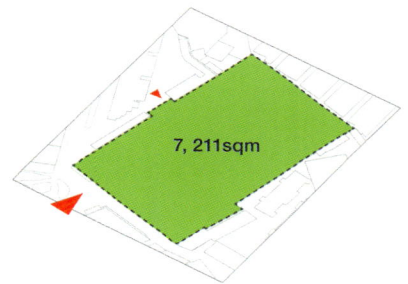

Site area and boundary

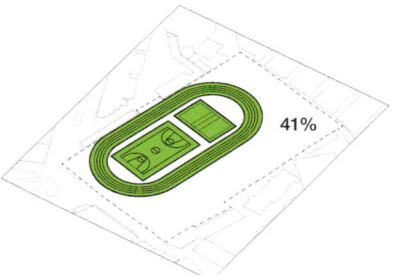

Sports facilities area

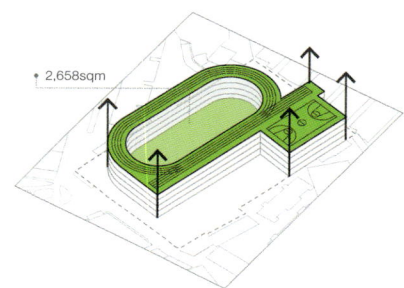

Mass extrusion

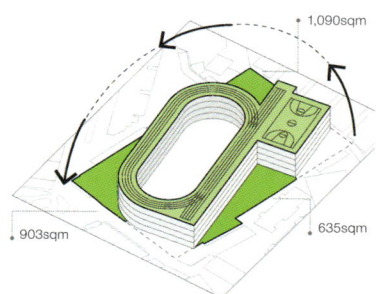

Mass rotation

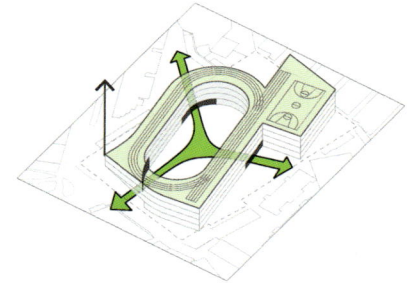

Ground space continuity

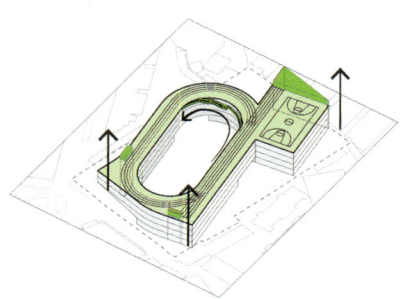

Vertical circulations

Design process diagram

Tai'an Dongximen Village Revitalization

Meng Fanhao + Zhu Peidong | line+ studio

Location: Dongximen Village, Tai'an, Shandong Province, China
Design firm: line+ studio
Principal architect: Meng Fanhao
Architecture design team: Tao Tao, Zhu Min, Xu Hao, Zhang Erjia, Huang Guangwei, Yuan Dong, Li Sanjian, Xie Yuting, Hao Jun, Xu Tianqu, Tu Dan
Interior design team: Zhu Jun, Jin Xin, Deng Hao, Zhang Sisi, Qiu Limin, Hu Jinwei, Zhou Xinyi, Zhang Ning, Wang Lijie
Landscape design team: Li Shangyang, Jin Jianbo, Chi Xiaomei, Su Chenjuan
Area: renovation—3,023 square meters, study and amenity—570 square meters
Design period: February 2019–August 2019
Construction period: May 2019–September 2020
Client: Lushang Pusu (Tai'an) Cultural Tourism Development Co. Ltd
Photography: zystudio, Pan Jie, Jin Xiaowen, line+ studio, Pan Bing
Model photography: Sun Lei, Pan Bing, line+ studio

Site plan

Rural Revitalization in the Age of New Media

Mount Tai, one of the Five Great Mountains of China, has carried great cultural significance since historical times. "Leaning against a cliff, I overlook all eight directions. All my eyes can see is calmness." In the words of the famous Chinese poet Li Bai, Mount Tai exhales the breath of the world and offers the most beautiful scenery on earth. Located at the foot of the Peak of the Nine Maidens, or Jiunvfeng, Dongximen Village is surrounded by mountains on all sides. Adjacent to the Shenlong Canyon, this village administrated by Tai'an City (Shandong Province) offers panoramic views of the gorge and the mountain peaks in the distance. Ironically, this magnificent natural scenery also hampered the development of Dongximen Village. Its isolation and the barrenness of the land caused the village to gradually lose touch with general economic progress. The young people of the village had left to work in the city, and only the elderly remained, resulting in a "hollowing-out" rural community—a growing phenomenon that China faces. This "hollowing-out" further aggravated the village's decay. There are dozens of villages in the Jiunvfeng area that share the same fate, but Dongximen Village is the most remotely located; it also faced the greatest challenges to its development.

In recent years, the countryside has become the focal point for Chinese architectural practice. In 2017, the Government's rural rejuvenation strategy had proposed in the 19th CPC National Congress report that rural development has become an issue of concern for all of society, starting with the top levels of government. That same year, a housing project in Dongziguan, Zhejiang Province—Dongziguan Affordable Housing—led by Meng Fanhao during his time at gad as the project principals, had gained popularity fast and achieved more than 1 billion clicks on social media platforms Wechat and Xiaohongshu as word spread online. The white-walled courtyard-style farmhouses evoked memories of a typical Jiangnan village, and the sustained media attention quickly turned Dongziguan Village into a popular destination. It not only prompted a return of young people who had previously left the village, but also attracted new inhabitants seeking to start businesses. The moment the abandoned village had been revived through the power of construction/buildings,

Aerial view © zystudio

line+ studio realized that in the Digital Age, architecture could act as a catalyst for the creation of value beyond its proper space.

In October 2018, the Shandong Lushang group had come to Zhejiang to inspect Dongziguan Village and a series of other rural projects of line+ studio in Hangzhou, Songyang, and Moganshan. After, they commissioned the studio for a rural rejuvenation project in Tai'an, Shandong Province. It was hoped that this project would have a similar impact as the Donziguan Affordable Housing project. One month later, the team arrived in Tai'an to inspect the site. The nineteen villages at the foot of Jiunvfeng were linked only by a winding, rugged mountain road. These villages were not only severely hollowed out, but also scattered. Faced with these challenges, line+ studio fast realized the importance of the project and determined how to best navigate it, guided by lessons from their past experiences. Based on their suggestion, the most remote village, Dongximen Village, eventually became the focal point for the overall rejuvenation of the villages.

Dongximen Village was a typical mountain village with dense vegetation and a small river running through it. If you were to climb to the nearby peak, you would be treated to spectacular views, and can even see Mount Tai in the distance. The project site was located in an abandoned area of the village—twelve dilapidated stone houses, some remaining stone walls, and a few farm buildings that had formerly been used as pig pens formed the initial context for the project. Due to the constraints of the land-use plan, the village didn't allow for an extension of the construction area, so the design scope was limited to the sites of the existing houses, prompting the questions: How can the remaining architectural structure stimulate the renewal of the village? And how can we deliver new growth potential for the sustainable development of the village?

To get around the many challenges of the project, line+ studio proposed a two-pronged design strategy. The first was through needle-like renovations: while maintaining the boundaries of the existing lots, the revitalization of the old village was achieved by taking the spatial stimulation of the surviving buildings and the ecological restoration of the environment as entry points. Second, visually expressive architecture was used as a medium to create media interest that could draw in visitors. This two-pronged strategy would jointly drive the overall development of Dongximen Village through the promotion of tourism.

Location has often been a constraint on rural development in the past, however, the dissemination prowess of the Internet has opened up the possibility of overcoming this limitation. Despite its benefits, this new trend prompts the fraternity to question how architecture and architects should respond to it. In the Dongximen Village renewal project, line+ studio sought to go beyond traditional architectural design, such as combining it with the specific social environment and policies; integrating resources from all levels; establishing a workflow from planning and design to construction, operation, and communication; and developing a model of innovation with design as the motor. In this way, architects become the node and link between various sectors, and evolve from "creators of space" to "enablers of space."

Dongximen Village before revitalization © line+ studio

Houses in Dongximen Village before revitalization © line+ studio

The Renewal of the Village

The remaining stone houses and walls in Dongximen Village were first carefully mapped and sorted through by line+ studio, identifying and preserving the better maintained parts, while the walls that could not be retained were dismantled and reused as building materials. The stones had undergone changes over time, giving them character and a certain reverence, and they became an important foundation, literally and symbolically, for "anchoring" the new buildings.

Stone buildings tend to have heavy walls and good insulation, but they also have the disadvantages of being costly, less waterproof, and less resistant to earthquakes.

Therefore, it became a priority for line+ studio to design stone buildings that met the needs of contemporary life based on the original materials and building form. Adding blockwork on the inside of the rubble walls, with insulation, waterproofing, and protective layers between them, enabled the traditional local stone wall masonry to finally satisfy contemporary usage requirements. This new structure has been inserted into the old rubble wall in the form of a steel frame. After considering the on-site construction conditions, line+ studio opted for the most commonly used I-beams as the decidedly appropriate material. The beams and columns are made of 200-by-200-millimeter I-beams, while the purlins are made of 100-by-148-millimeter I-beams. Rigid joints, which provide greater structural strength, are used in between the main frames and the purlins and are lap-jointed to the main frames. While facilitating construction from a technical aspect, this also paid homage to traditional Chinese wood frames.

This frame system is made flexible enough to respond to the complex site characteristics of the old houses by applying linear, L-shaped and U-shaped layouts accordingly. The small-scale frames formed the corridors, while the large-scale frames became rooms. In a sense, this way of generating units from basic frames, and then expanding those units into a whole, is analogous to the way traditional settlements are composed.

Courtyard No. 1 © zystudio

Courtyards No. 1, 2 and 4:
The existing structures were newly built stone houses. The design preserves part of their rubble walls and organized the relationship between the buildings and the site. Courtyard No. 1 is formed around a tree, while courtyards No. 2 and No. 4 form an L-shape.

Courtyard No. 3:
On the site stood a few small auxiliary stone houses which were used for storage and production in the past. The design utilizes the existing rubble masses and connects them with glass boxes. Each of the stone boxes hosts a bathroom, bedroom, and other facilities, while the glass box serves as a shared space for children to play in.

Courtyard No. 5:
The existing building had two parts arranged parallel to each other, running north to south. The south side hosted a new elongated stone house built by the farmers, but it was too long. The design breaks up the existing volume and divides it into two parts. The building on the west side retains its original linear layout, forming two guestrooms. On the east side, a vertical volume was inserted in line with the topography to create a public space on the ground floor that serves the guestrooms. Additionally, large steps were set up inside according to the terrain, to form a multilayered and multifunctional interior space.

Courtyard No. 6:
The plot is located close to the main road leading up the hill, so it was decided that it would function as a gathering space. Considering its different purpose, and based on metal plates as the main material, the design concept of "folding" was adopted to form a continuous entity of walls, roofs, and railings. It has also been blended with the steps to resolve the height difference of the site, giving the whole building exterior a light origami look.

Courtyards No. 7, 8 and 9:
The existing buildings were all old residential houses with an enclosed layout. The new buildings follow their architectural texture and spatial form, enclosing a central courtyard by adding and subtracting volumes from the original spatial logic. These courtyard spaces integrate indoor and outdoor areas and changes in elevation. The ancient trees on the site of courtyard No. 8 were also left untouched. The structural framework has been flexibly expanded around it, thus creating a courtyard under the shade of a tree, as well as a multifunctional internal space.

Courtyard No. 10:
The existing building had an L-shaped layout. The design follows the original spatial pattern and adopts an L-shape similar to that of courtyard No. 5 to envelop a courtyard. The entrance ascends along with the terrain, forming an outdoor platform that rises above the to establish a dialog with the distant mountains.

Courtyard No. 11:
The existing buildings were constructed in

Entrance of Courtyard No. 3 © Pan Jie

Courtyard No. 6 © zystudio

recent years, with a north–south alignment and a 3-meter height difference between the front and back rows. The design preserves the spatial layout of the original buildings and resolves the height difference between the front and rear buildings. The partial enlargement of the roof provides a new, shared public space and roof terrace.

Courtyard No. 12:
The plot is located in the westernmost area of the project site. Given its relative isolation, the design turned it into a stand-alone guesthouse. The existing structure was an old residential building that had fallen into a state of disrepair. The new building retains the old rubble walls and inserts a two-story steel structure with a gable roof. The sloping roof is covered with simple, flat cement tiles. Courtyard No. 12 presents itself as a lighter structure with a large L-shaped gray space overhanging the second floor, which blends in with the surrounding native trees to converse with nature.

Courtyard No. 8 © zystudio

Courtyard No. 12 © zystudio

Restaurant © zystudio

1. Before renovation © line+ studio
2. After renovation © zystudio

In addition to this sequence of mainly residential courtyard-centered spaces, line+ studio also renovated and updated the old pigpen and three private houses, inserting new architectural functions one by one—a reception area, café, and a restaurant.

The abandoned pigpen is separated from the planned parking lot by a stream, and provides good accessibility, thus serving as a reception area for the new buildings. The light steel structure used on the site gives new life to an old space, with a large-scale pitched roof and a permeable spatial interface, emphasizing the invisibility of the building volume among the natural environment, and the fluidity between the indoor and outdoor spaces. Environmentally friendly and natural burnt cedar shingles have been elegantly arranged on the roof, echoing the surrounding lush vegetation. The other two residential buildings situated in the middle of the hill are backed by mountains and provide a panoramic view. The prefabricated light steel structure transforms them into a restaurant. The rubble walls and glass curtain walls open up to different views of the landscape, dissolving the building into the mountain scenery to provide an immersive dining experience.

Between the courtyards and the new buildings, a meandering walkway and landscape experience has been created. line+ studio aimed to incorporate the rich and varied natural environment into the design of the footpaths, enhancing the perception of the settlement and the environment through the motion of the body. Coming from the outside, visitors walk through scattered forests along wooden bridges and stone steps; they climb, look up, turn, and finally ascend to the top, to catch a glimpse of the natural wilderness to the north, forming a narrative experience from the beginning to the end; from low to high, and high to low. A large number of stones showing traces of the old village have been reused to pave stone paths, steps, and low walls, continuing to chronicle the growth of the new village. When it came to plant selection, the integrity of the forest was maintained and a diversity in plant selection was achieved by replanting Chinese hackberry, Chinese photinia, and Chinese fountain grass, to complement the large native trees on the site.

View toward the reception/café © zystudio

1. The abandoned pigpen before renovation © line+ studio
2. The pigpen after renovation © zystudio

Ground-floor plan

1. Pavilion
2. Reception/café
3. Restaurant
4. Multifunction room
5. Guestroom with a children's space
6. Guestroom
7. Bridge
8. Parking lot
9. Jiunvfeng Study
10. Jiunvfeng Bubble Pool

Ground-floor plan of courtyards No. 1 to No. 12
(the stone walls that were retained are highlighted in red)

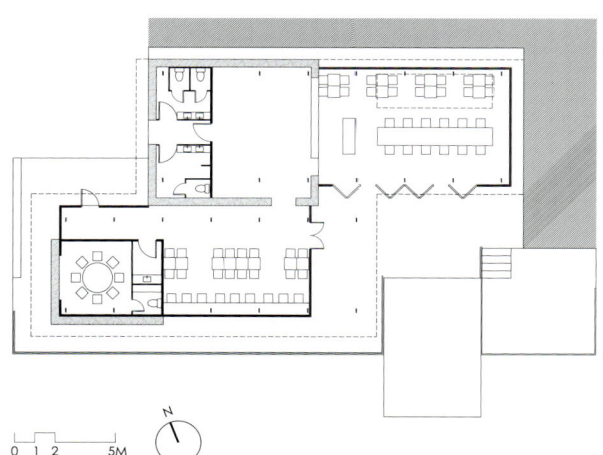

Restaurant—ground-floor plan

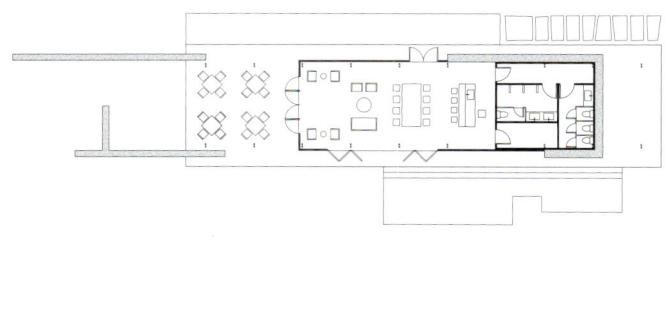

Reception/café—ground-floor plan

Aerial view of Jiunvfeng Study © Jin Xiaowen

Jiunvfeng Study

As a building designed to attract media attention, Jiunvfeng Study on Mount Tai is located on the top of a scenic mountain ridge. Driving up the sloping mountain road, the Study can be easily spotted, having the mountains to its east and the village to its rear. The main idea for the design of the Study was to create a highly distinctive "white space" that sits on the top of the rugged mountain ridge in the north.

The building's structure is divided into three parts from top to bottom: a white "cloud," transparent glass center, and a heavy rubble-wall base. To the north, it overlooks a permeable interface of canyons and peaks. The long and narrow path at the entrance connects the café and reading areas at either end of the building, blurring the boundary between the structure and the natural landscape to give visitors the illusion of being in a mountaintop forest. A structural system of light steel and membranes chosen for the main building allows the design to follow the profile of the mountain range, thereby acquiring a seemingly weightless shape.

The entrance of the building lies on the south side, toward the village, placed in such a way as to indicate the general orientation of the building in relation to the site. Its walls are made of local rubble, which is heavy and solid, almost as if it is merging with the mountain; a curved interface guides visitors inside. As path winds and turns, panoramic views of the canyon and the mountains become visible through glass panes that seem to extend endlessly, framed by a space formed by a series of arched, light steel joists of gradually changing dimensions. The transparent glass interface not only allows the external landscape to enter the space, but it also conceals the physical structure hoisting the roof. From afar, Jiunvfeng Study appears like a cloud resting gently on top of the mountain rocks.

Curved glass curtain wall extends toward the mountains © zystudio

Entrance to the Jinuvfeng Study © zystudio

Jiunvfeng Study interior © Jin Xiaowen

The construction of the study began in April 2019 and was completed in September 2019. During the construction process, the precise and fast assembly of the prefabricated light steel construction modules ensured a timely completion.

Foundation:
In order to achieve the desired floating effect, the foundation was raised slightly higher than the surrounding ground. After surveying the terrain, lighting conditions, and landscape features at the site, it was found that the height and density of the canopy of the surrounding vegetation directly affected the positioning of the foundation and the viewing height of the building. Therefore, the foundation height was readjusted to 400 millimeters.

Main structure:
The prefabricated modular components guaranteed the accuracy of construction. Steel columns that are 150 millimeters thick support a curved girder, on top of which twenty-eight pairs of arched double joists have been erected. The sequence of gradually changing, densely arranged arched joists allows for the smooth application of the interior and exterior membranes.

Interior and exterior membranes:
Wire mesh is attached in between the twenty-eight pairs of arched joists, on top of which evenly laid out tin foil reflects the light from the LED strips, while encapsulated isolation is laid and fixed above the tin foil. Fixed to the lower side of the joists, the inner membrane is made of a translucent fabric, which is carefully suspended and tensioned with metal clasps.

Rubble walls:
The south entrance and wall façade are built with local rubble and tied together with small steel columns. For this, the team selected appropriately sized colored stones from the site and guided the local construction team in completing the masonry work.

Lighting and interior design:
LED light strips are arranged longitudinally above the lower joists. In order to achieve a uniform lighting effect on a large area of the interior membrane, several experiments with different arrangements and illumination levels, as well as different intervals of the LED light strips, were carried out on-site.

Section model

Membrane roof © Jin Xiaowen

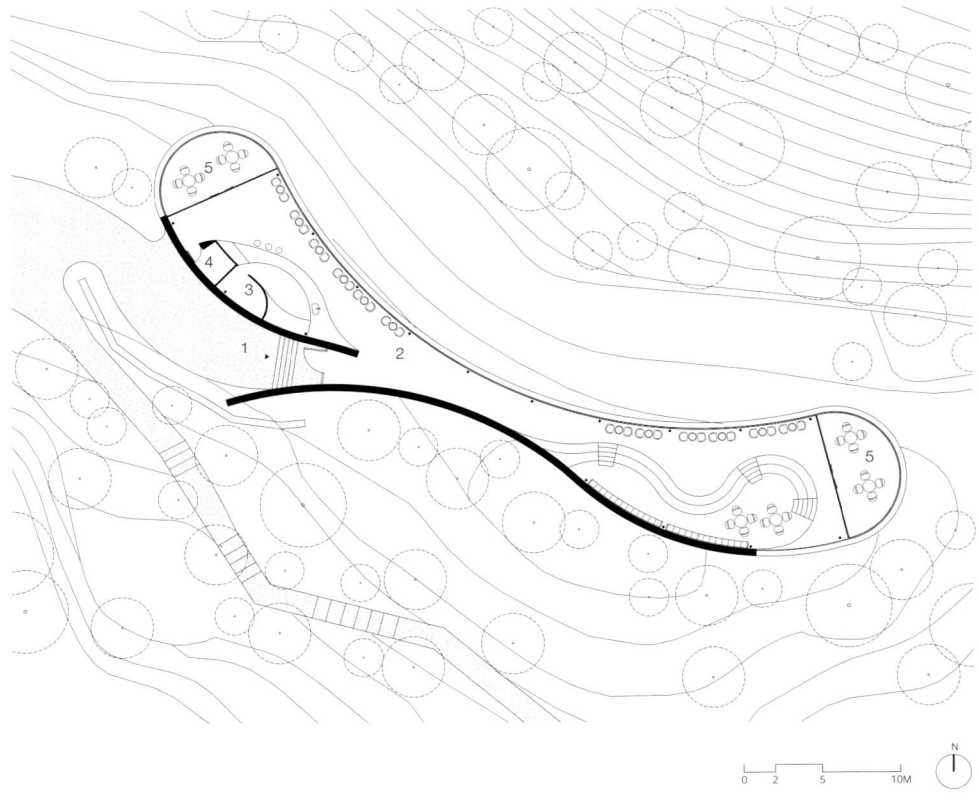

Ground-floor plan

1. Entrance
2. Book bar
3. Counter
4. Restroom
5. Balcony

Exploded axonometric diagram

1. Outer membrane surface: Valmex Mehgies 1,050 g/m^2

2. Outer keel: 80x80x2.5 mm square tube frame
   Insulation cotton encapsulation
   Stretched steel wire mesh
   Tin foil padding

3. Inner keel: 80x80x2.5 mm square tube frame
   LED light strip

4. White frosted lightbox membrane
   Silver strip for lightbox membrane

5. 60 mm cast-in-site terrazzo floor
   40 mm floor heating layer
   30 mm insulation layer
   Waterproof layer
   20 mm cement mortar leveling layer
   Steel mixed structure layer

6. Local ashlar masonry
   Steel column
   30 mm insulation layer
   Half brick wall
   Leveling layer
   White texture painting

7. 12+12 mm curved surface ultra-white laminated glass
   D100 steel column sprayed with white fluorocarbon

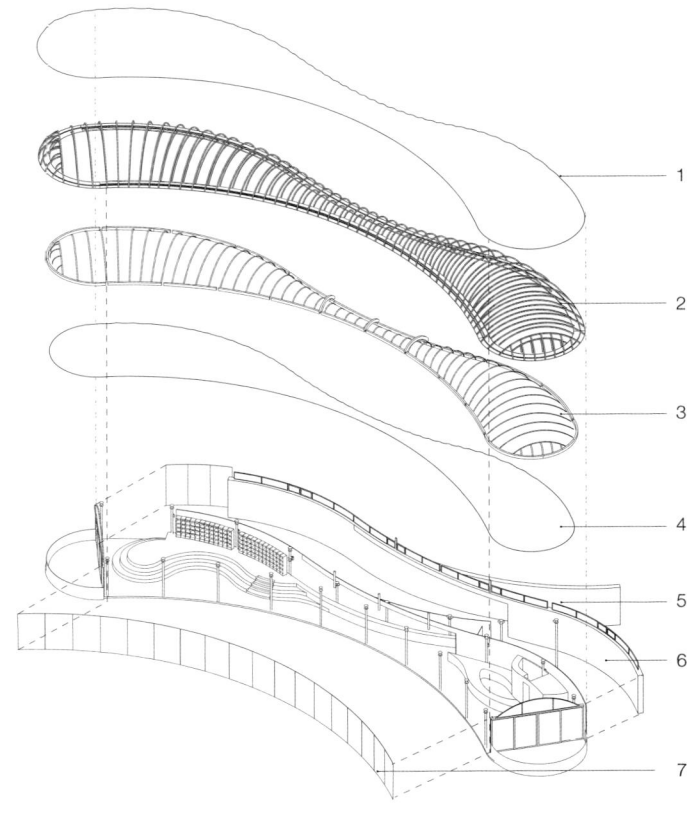

Aerial view of Jiunvfeng Bubble Pool and Study © zystudio

Jiunvfeng Bubble Pool

Like Jiunvfeng Study, Jinuvfeng Bubble Pool also serves as an instrument to attract visitors. If the Study is a "cloud" located at the top of the mountains, then the Bubble Pool and its supporting facilities are like shells scattered in the hillside of the village to echo the vast and magnificent forest scenery. As one walks through the entrance of the village, past the guesthouses arranged along the hillside, and up the path made of local stones, the pure white Bubble Pool slowly emerges from the mountainous vegetation.

The Bubble Pool and its supporting facilities are divided into three areas: dressing rooms, a sea bathing section, and a fitness area, which make up three building volumes. To the west, sits the semi-outdoor sea bath. To ensure the flow and permeability of the pool building, it was essential to create an unspoiled space without pillars and visual obstructions. This intention fashions a 10-meter-high pure white roof that rises from the ground in an open and airy shape, projecting toward the distant mountains. Sheltering the pool area within, it displays a rising form that maximizes the landscape views for visitors relaxing in the water. On the east side lies the indoor area serving the pool, characterized by a smaller, more restrained arch shape. It hosts the reception, dressing rooms, showers, and a small sauna. To the south, in the third volume, is the fitness studio, which faces the village and the foot of the mountain; enclosed in the shell, yet still partially visible because of its design character, it draws curious gazes and invites people to enter, to discover the secrets and joys that reside within. From a distance, Jiunvfeng Bubble Pool looks like precious shells lost in Mount Tai's sea of clouds. The spaces enclosed by the three curved surfaces were born naturally. By incorporating the local landscape and following the topography of the mountain, they establish a balanced connection between nature and the village.

Shell-like space © zystudio

Entrance to the gym © zystudio

View toward the mountains © zystudio

The construction of the Bubble Pool took into account the purity and simplicity of the space, balancing the relationship between the building, the landscape, and the interior, while simplifying the structure and materials as much as possible.

Frame:
Overhanging the pool by 10 meters, the roof is made of prefabricated curved steel joists. With the help of precise modeling and calculation, the vertical and horizontal joists meet high in the air, while being firmly fixed on the foundation, making the structure durable and easy to install.

Surface:
After the main frame of the building made of steel joists was built, an external insulation layer was added and then covered with a stainless-steel surface, combining high plasticity, toughness, and mechanical strength. Through highly accurate joints and meticulous polishing, a smooth and seamless appearance is achieved, providing the basis for the free-flowing form.

Finishing:
A coherent metallic-white spray paint for the interior and exterior of the building ensures the integrity of the building. Combined with large floor-to-ceiling glass walls and highly reflective glass, a pure and transparent look and feel is created.

Pool © zystudio

Aerial view of Jiunvfeng Bubble Pool © zystudio

Ground-floor plan

1. Entrance
2. Gym
3. Dressing room
4. Pool

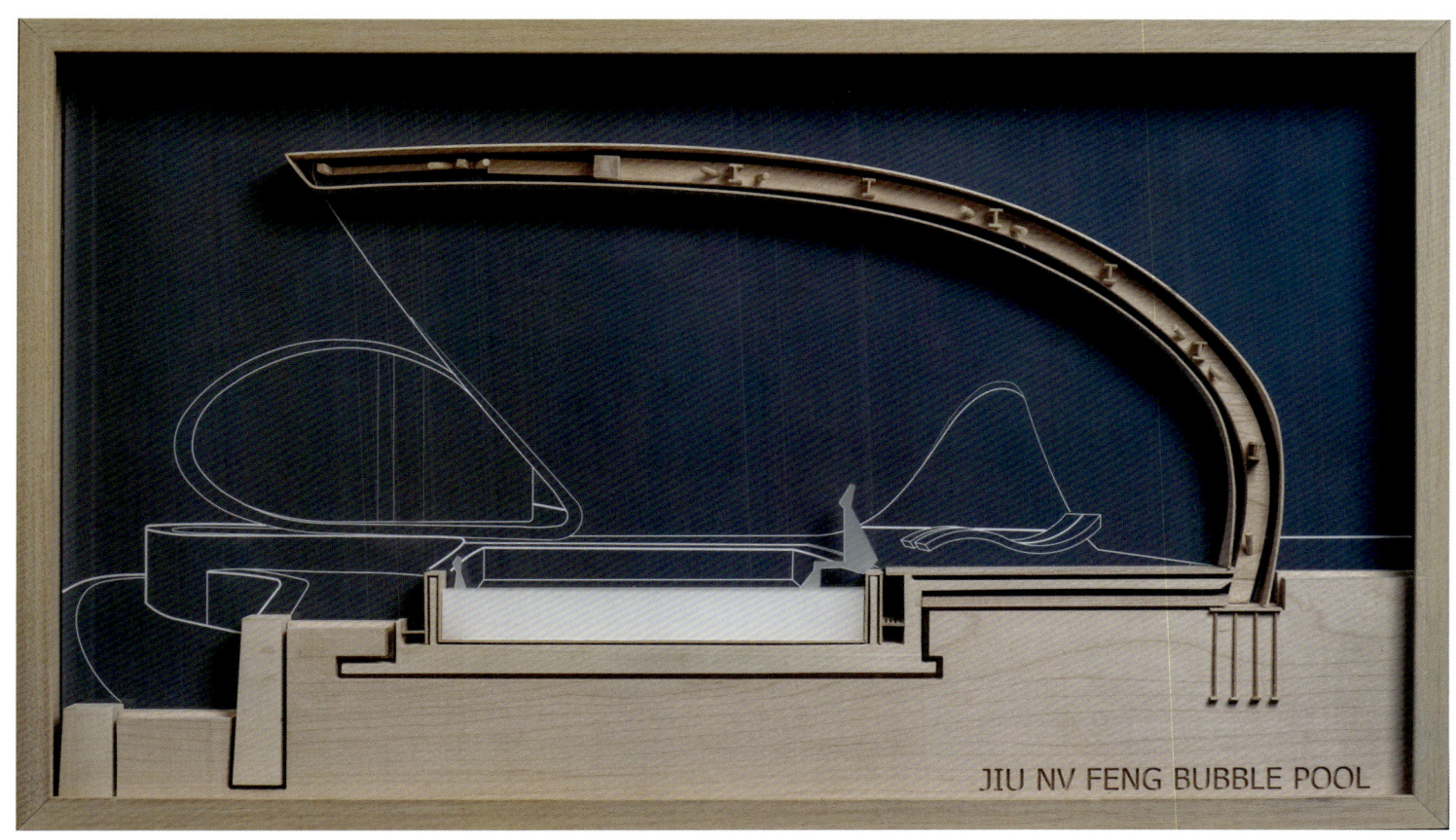

Section model

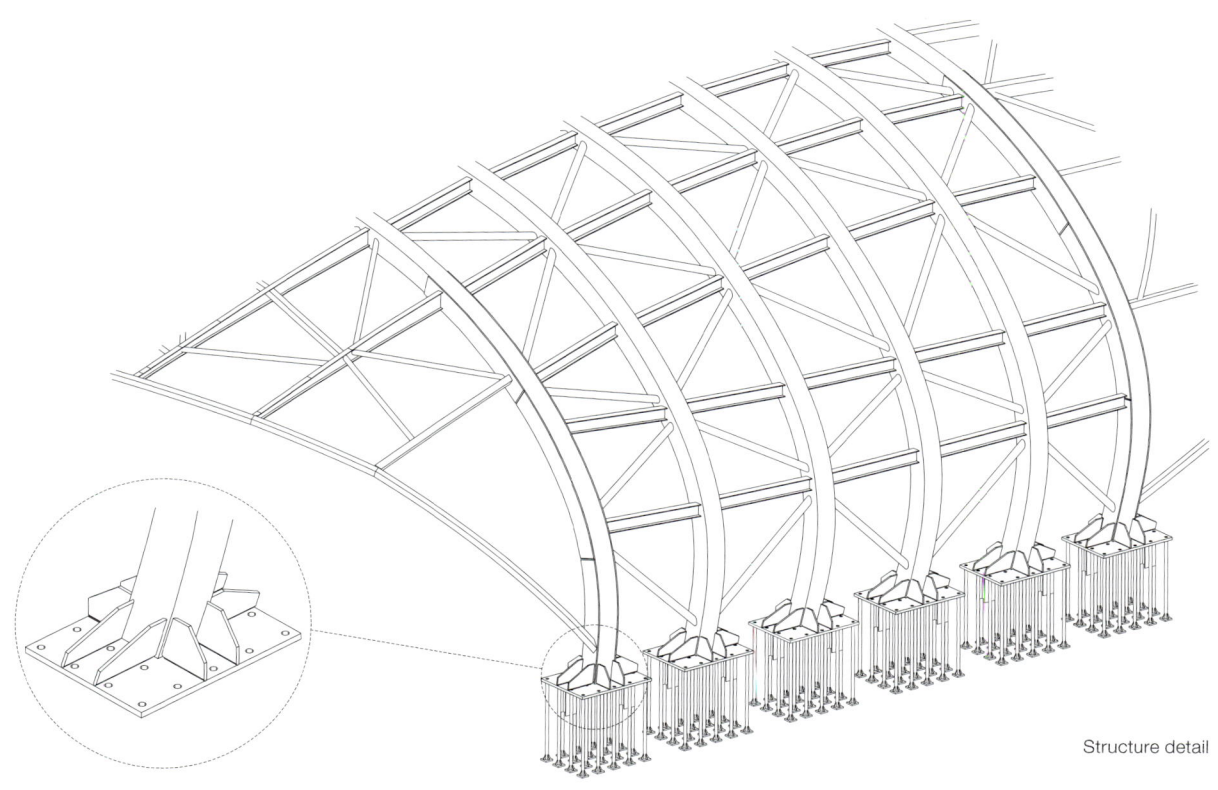

Structure detail

Tourists driving to visit the project during the Labor Day holiday © Pan Bing

Architecture as Agent

When the whole project went into operation in October 2020, the Jiunvfeng Study and Bubble Pool quickly became popular photo destinations, thanks to the Internet, just as the team had envisioned. During the Chinese autumn holiday season, the project as a whole generated a revenue of more than 1 million yuan (US$153,000), which indirectly benefited local businesses as tourists flocked to the area. As a typical rural rejuvenation project, in which a focal point drives the overall development—while being jointly supported by the local government and state-level funds—the revitalization and modernization of Dongximen Village achieved a reorganization of resources through architecture. In this process, demands from different stakeholders had to be met: the Government sought to explore a model for rural rejuvenation; the financiers sought to maximize the return on their investment; and the villagers sought to improve their quality of life and increase their income. In turn, the architects not only had to focus on their own disciplinary expertise, such as village types and construction techniques, but also acted as mediators to maximize the allocation of resources and achieve a win-win situation for all parties involved.

Media and social media coverage of the project © CCTV

Media and social media coverage of the project © CCTV and CGTN

Village aerial view © ZY Architecture photography

Summer 2025 101

The Chuan Malt Whisky Distillery

Lyndon Neri + Rossana Hu | Neri&Hu Design and Research Office

Location: Emeishan, Sichuan Province, China
Architect: Neri&Hu Design and Research Office
Principal architect: Lyndon Neri, Rossana Hu
Associate director in charge: Nellie Yang
Associate: Utsav Jain, Siyu Chen
Design team: Feng Wang, Guo Peng, Josh Murphy, Fergus Davis, Alexandra Heijink, Vivian Bao, Yota Takaira, Rosie Tseng, Nicolas Fardet, Yin Sheng, Lili Cheng, July Huang, Luna Hong, Haiou Xin
FF&E design: Design Republic
Landscape design: YIYU Design
Experience design: BRC Imagination Arts
Construction (architecture & landscape): Qi'an Group, Suzhou Hezhan
Construction (interior): K&H International
Gross floor area: 7,350 square meters
Completion: October 2021
Client: Pernod Ricard Group
Photography: Chen Hao

Aerial view

For over a thousand years, the majestic Mount Emei, rising over a thousand feet in the Emeishan region, has stood as one of the most deeply spiritual places in China, even gaining UNESCO World Heritage Site classification in 1996. Claiming the mystical mountain peaks as a backdrop, the project site holds as much reverence. Through the centuries, the land has been an impressive monastery, the site of several historic battles, and a stopping point for pilgrims, as well as merchants traveling along ancient trade routes. While no built remnants of the past remain on the site, the architects opine that "its very emptiness is powerfully suggestive of all of its fabled memories."

The rich history and mysticism of the site and surrounding landscape naturally were a source of influence for the design of The Chuan, the first malt whisky venture into China of French wine and spirits seller Pernod Ricard. In 2018 the architects won the international design competition to construct this distillery and headquarters for the brand and jumped at the opportunity to create something "timeless" that would sustain material and cultural heritage as well as speak to the core value of the brand.

The site, surrounded on three sides by a winding creek, with Mount Emei in the background, exemplifies the Chinese notion *shan-shui*—the duality of natural elements that make up the world we live in. *Shan-shui* translates literally to "mountain-water," with *shan* representing strength and permanence, and *shui* representing fluidity and transformation; they are two opposing yet complementary forces.

In the spirit of this philosophy, the architects strike a balance between architecture and landscape, and "mountain" and "water" with a design that draws strength from its humbleness and simplicity as it manifests this duality through graceful yet impactful volumes—the distillery's industrial buildings stand as modern interpretations of vernacular Chinese architecture and the visitor experience buildings appear as elemental geometries grounded in the terrain.

Architecture coexisting with the landscape

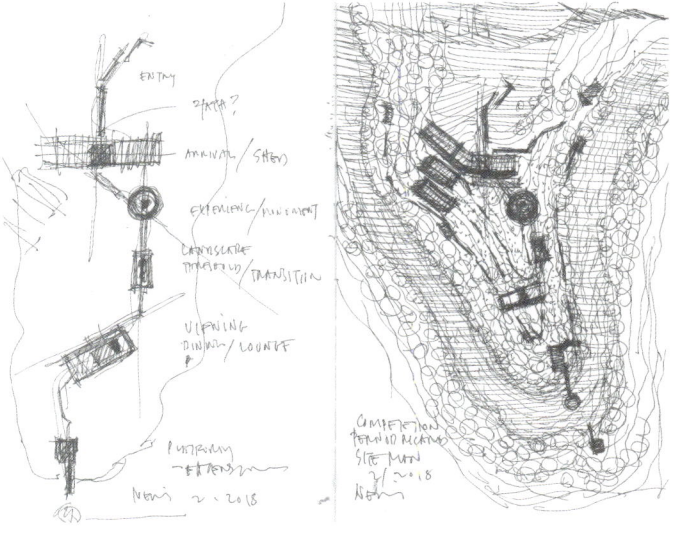

Conceptual sketches

Experience center

Experience center in the landscape

Whisky production facilities are house in three long buildings situated at the north side of the site; parallel in formation, they are tucked into the natural gentle slope of the land with gradually descending rooflines. Reclaimed clay tiles interpret the region's vernacular architecture and create an unpretentious, humble appearance on the buildings' pitched roofs that rest, in contrast, on modern post-and-beam structures. The infill of the rock walls is made from the very boulders extracted from the ground during site leveling, so that, according to the architects, "the cycle of destruction and recreation may continue in permanent evolution."

In contrast to the vernacular roots of the industrial buildings, the two visitor experience buildings are built upon fundamental geometries, specifically the circle and the square, which in Chinese philosophy represent heaven and earth, respectively. The round "tasting experience" building is partially submerged in the ground, with five subterranean tasting rooms surrounding a domed courtyard that contains a cascading water feature in the middle. The upper part of the dome reveals itself slightly above ground in three concentric brick rings that subtly mirrors the silhouette of Mount Emei. This sculptural landform takes stage as an iconic presence that can be seen from every part the site. It also acts as a finishing destination for visitors, from which they can enjoy a panoramic vistas. The square restaurant and bar building is located further down the topography, cantilevered on two sides with one corner hovering over the riverbank. The dining space is organized along the building's perimeter to gain breathtaking, open views, and at the core an open-air courtyard is oriented to frame the Emei peak as a borrowed scene.

Besides a deep appreciation for the site's natural resources, the project is also an embodiment of the exquisite artistry woven into whisky making and blending, which is in dialogue with traditional Chinese craftsmanship and knowledge of materials. A variety of concrete, cement, and stone mixtures form the base material palette of the distillery and find resonance in the strong mineral presence of the site. Accent finishes are drawn from those used in the whisky craft, such as the copper distillation pots and aged oak casks. In this project, the architects strove to always embody the duality and dichotomy of the concept of *shan-shui*. In The Chuan, elements exist in opposition yet complement each other, to create a harmonious balance between surroundings and structure.

Water courtyard

	2	1. Under the eaves
1	3	2. VIP room
		3. Tasting room

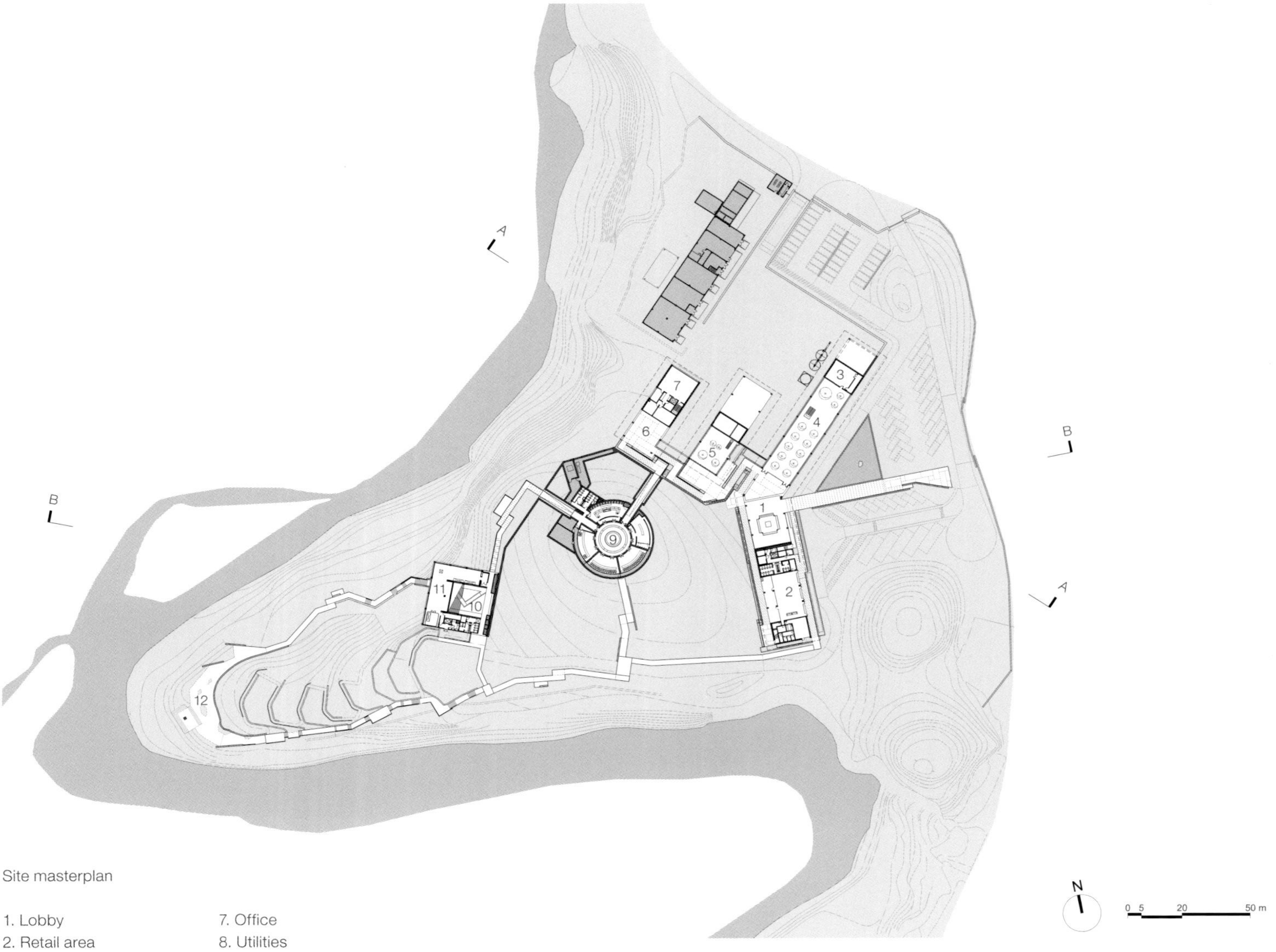

Site masterplan

1. Lobby
2. Retail area
3. Milling
4. Fermentation
5. Distillation
6. Cooperage
7. Office
8. Utilities
9. Experience center
10. Water courtyard
11. Restaurant and bar
12. Landscape walk

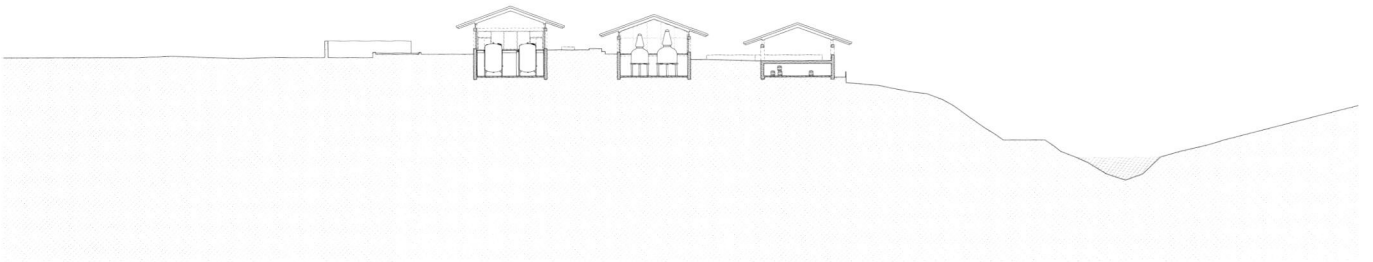

Site section A

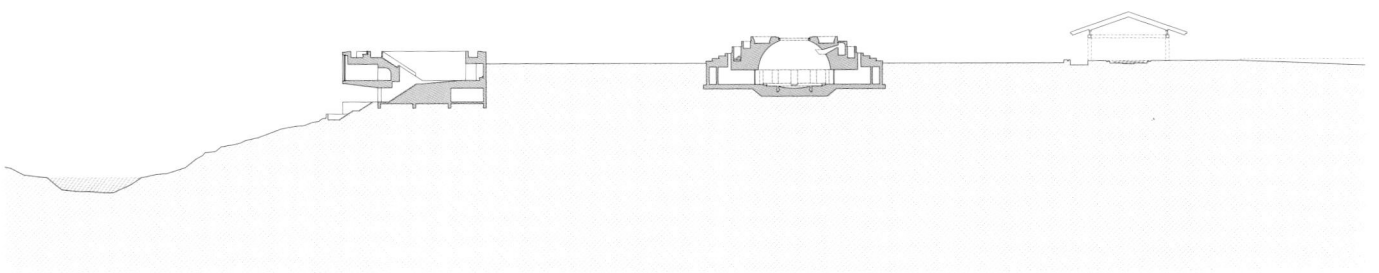

Site section B

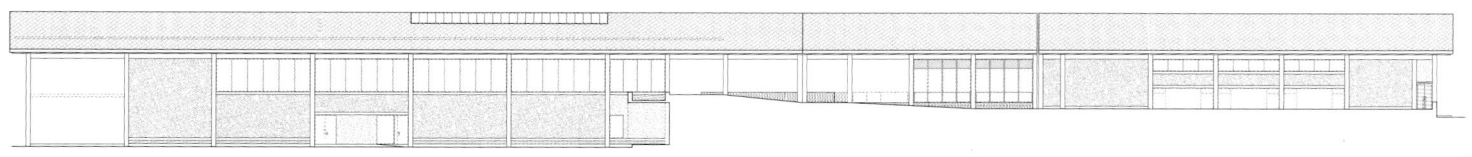

West elevation—distillery

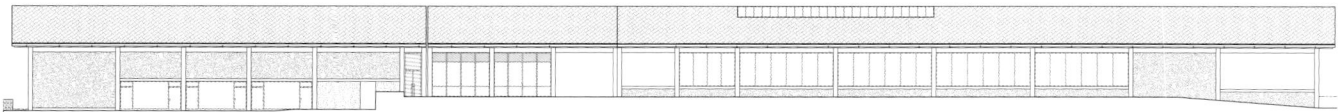

East elevation—distillery

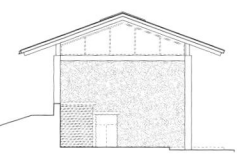 

North elevation—distillery   South elevation—distillery

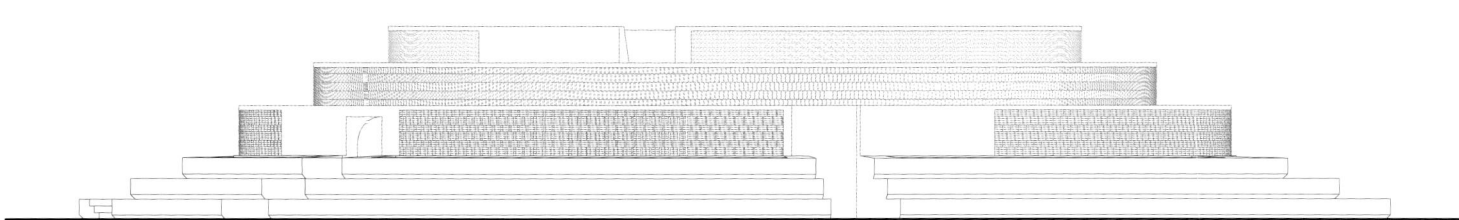

Experience center—south elevation

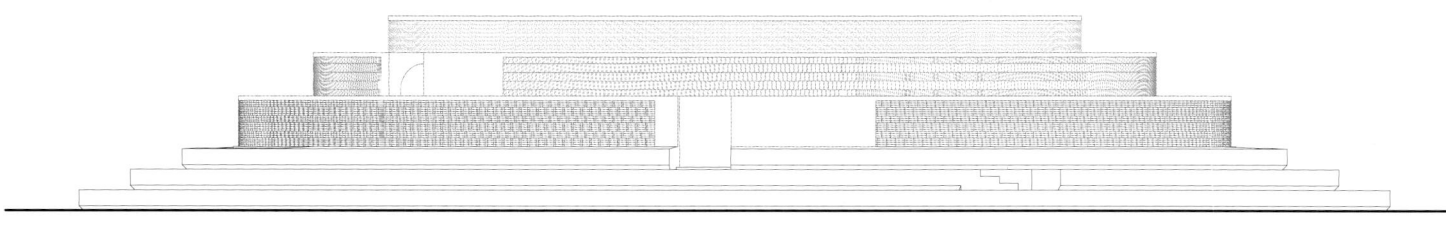

Experience center—north elevation

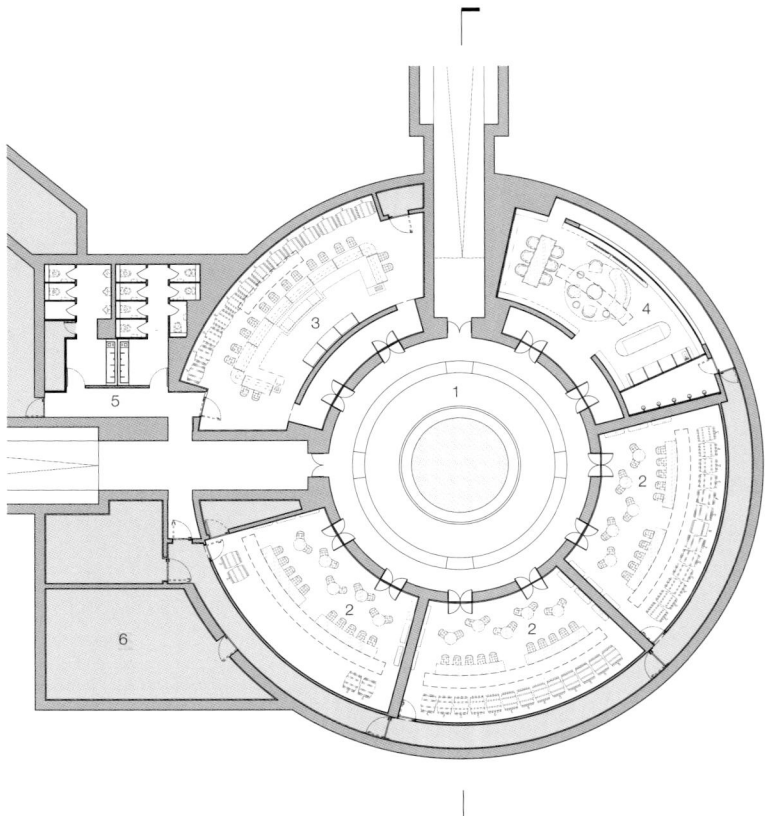

Experience center floor plan

1. Courtyard
2. Tasting room
3. Blending/cocktail
4. VIP
5. Restrooms
6. Prep room

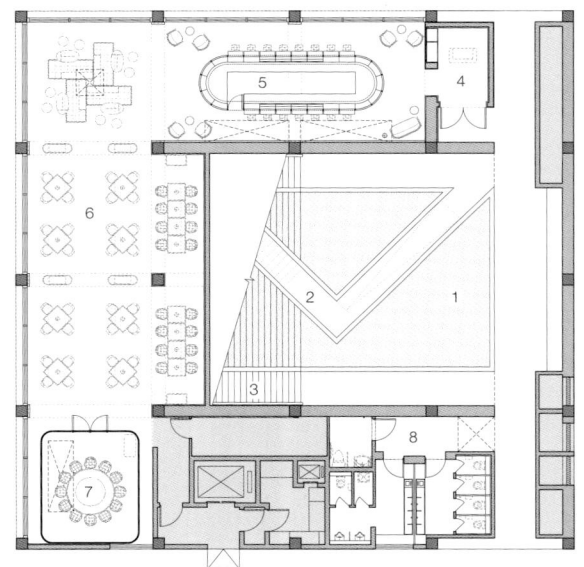

Restaurant floor plan

1. Water courtyard
2. To landscape walk
3. To roof terrace
4. Reception
5. Bar
6. Restaurant
7. Private dining
8. Restrooms

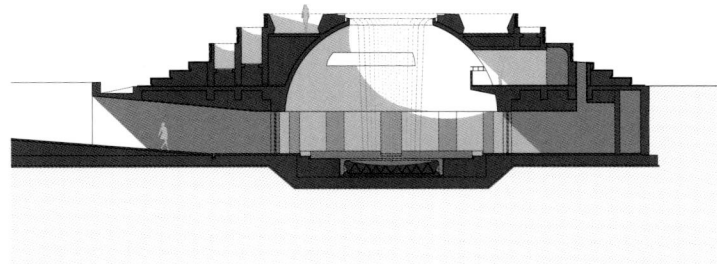

Experience center section

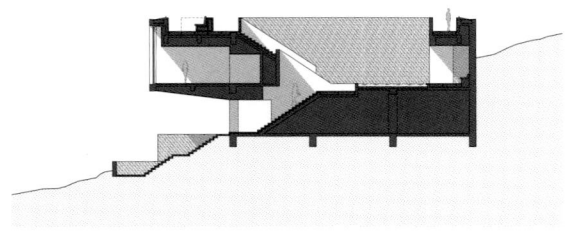

Restaurant and bar section

Wall section

1. Self-leveling concrete floor
2. Double glazing window
3. Cement board
4. Cast-in-situ concrete structure
5. Natural stone cladding
6. Natural stone
7. Interior wall finish
8. Insulation layer
9. Concrete block wall
10. Metal louvers with window
11. Steel structure
12. Wood finish aluminum panels
13. Concrete roof deck
14. Insulation board
15. Waterproofing layer
16. Recycled and new clay roof tiles
17. Copper metal fascia
18. Dark-gray metal fascia

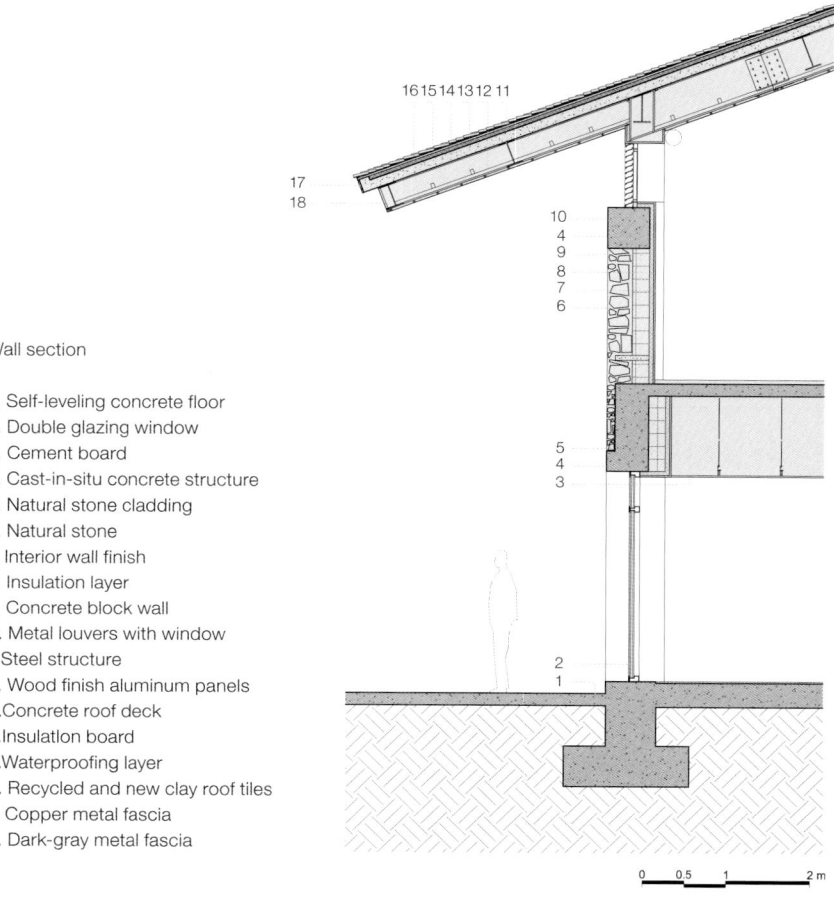

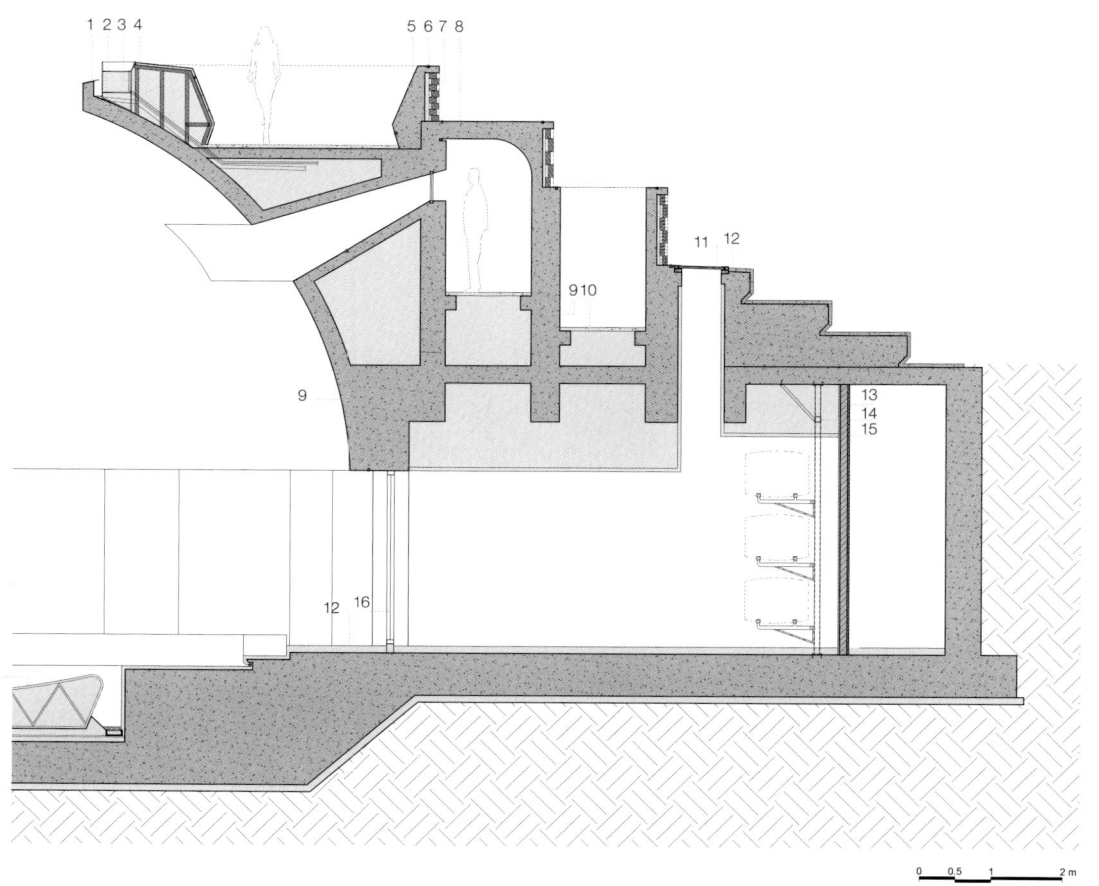

Wall section

1. Water spout
2. Metal tray for water feature
3. Steel structure
4. Precast smooth concrete
5. Cast-in-situ smooth concrete
6. Lightning copper strip
7. Brick masonry
8. Recessed LED strip
9. Cast-in-situ concrete structure
10. Precast aggregate concrete
11. Double glazing skylight
12. Cast-in-situ aggregate concrete
13. Dry wall with finish
14. Metal structure for barrels
15. Cement board with finish
16. Solid wood door
17. Copper bowl for water feature

798CUBE Art Museum

Zhu Pei | Studio Zhu Pei

Location: Beijing, China
Architect: Studio Zhu Pei
Principal architect: Zhu Pei
Design team: Shuhei Nakamura, You Changchen, Zhang Shun, Liu Ling, Wang Liyan, Jia Bin, Ding Xinyue, Chang Jiang
Structural and MEP team: The Design Institute of Landscape & Architecture China Academy of Art
Lighting design team: Ning Field Lighting Design CO., LTD.
Main contractor: Handan Second Building Institute Co., LTD.
Gross floor area: 3,540 square meters
Design period: 2015–2016
Completion: December 2020
Client: Beijing Qixing Huadian Science and Technology CO., LTD.
Photography: Jin Weiqi, Zhu Runzi, Studio Zhu Pei

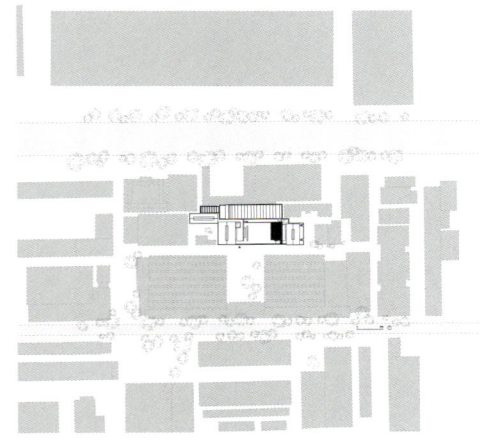

Site plan

798CUBE Art Museum, a renovation project by Studio Zhu Pei, creates the impression of concrete blocks that have been placed within Beijing's 798 Art District, the city's new art and cultural landmark zone. The museum sits adjacent to the Pace Art Museum and the Minsheng Museum of Modern Art, were also designed by the Studio in 2009 and 2016 separately. The idea of the art museum begins with a sensitive and in-depth observations of the surroundings, with the intention to retain as many of the original industrial buildings as possible. To that end, new buildings have been inserted to create tension between the old and new, allowing them to complement each other and showcase the industrial heritage of the area—it was originally built in the 1950s to house military factories in China.

Before renovation © Studio Zhu Pei

View from the main entrance looking toward the courtyard © Zhu Runzi

View of the main entrance © Zhu Runzi

Close-up view of concrete wall © Zhu Runzi

The design of the art museum traces the texture of the original industrial buildings, adopting a series of concrete cubes to shape the order of orthogonal geometric shapes and reflect the construction and planning logic of the 798 Art District. The original square, surrounded on three sides by industrial buildings is transformed into a relatively closed central courtyard with the help of an independent cast-in-situ concrete wall. The huge steel beam sliding crane spans the concrete walls from north to south. It can not only support art installations structurally but is also a mechanical traction device with naturally sagging tensioned canvas that has a shape similar to reverse arches. To suit the weather and sun angle, this reversed-arch-shaped canvas can be opened or closed to facilitate shading or rain protection.

Courtyard © Zhu Runzi

112 Architecture China

Mechanical traction device opened © Zhu Runzi

Mechanical traction device with reverse-arch canvas © Jin Weiqi

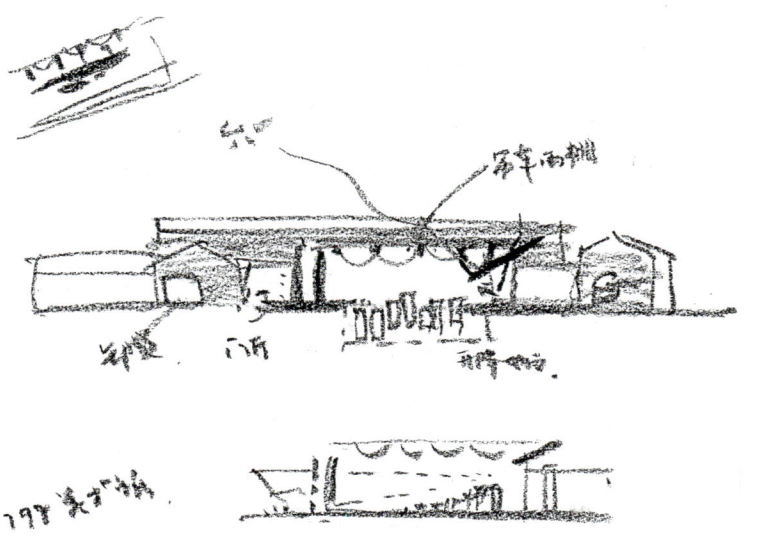
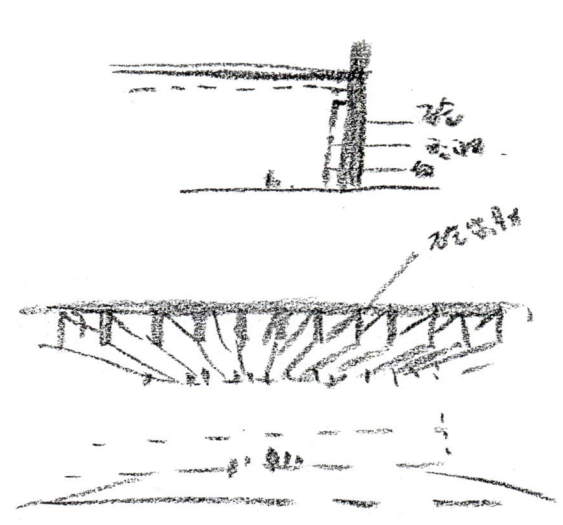

Conceptual sketch

Main exhibition space © Jin Weiqi

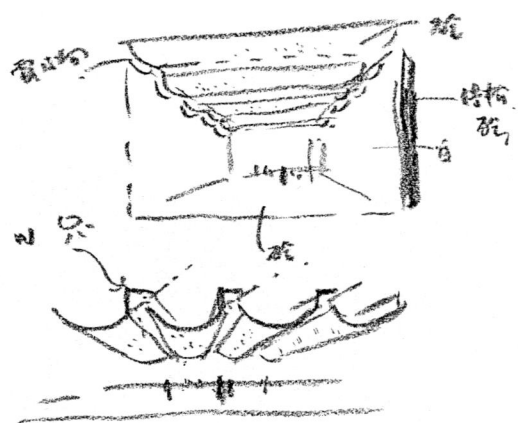

Main exhibition space sketch

114 Architecture China

Multifunction space suited for exhibitions and lectures © Zhu Runzi

Lobby © Zhu Runzi

Stair © Jin Weiqi

The café, and bookstore with its transparent glass curtain wall, face west toward the courtyard. A machine installation between the roof and the wall can be rotated at any angle so that in summer it can be rotated into a sloping wall to block the strong afternoon sun, and in winter it can be rotated into a horizontal roof to let the warm afternoon sunshine into the area. In addition, the free-standing concrete walls are installed with horizontally movable gates to facilitate the transport of oversized art installations. The concrete floor of the courtyard is divided into strips, and each of them can be raised or lowered according to different requirements. Thus, the courtyard has the potential to be transformed either into an outdoor theater with gradually rising seating or an outdoor exhibition space with a staggered, floating, island-like exhibition booth. The variability and flexibility make the courtyard a place for people to gather, an ideal venue to host the opening ceremony, or an outdoor theater and outdoor exhibition space with shade from the sun and rain.

Atrium © Jin Weiqi

The design explores the expressiveness of column-free, horizontally extended structural forms and materials. Both newly constructed galleries feature column-free, large-span cast-in-place concrete structures. One features massive inverted-arch curved beams, and the other uses a concrete close-ribbed large-span beam structural system.

The museum design also captures the material characteristics of the industrial buildings in the 798 Art District using cast-in-situ concrete and red brick as the main materials. It highlights the construction characteristics of the intersection and transformation of these two materials, especially through the structural form and the enclosure wall, which embody the unique tectonic culture of the industrial buildings in the 798 Art District.

Loading dock and storage © Zhu Runzi

Model detail © Studio Zhu Pei

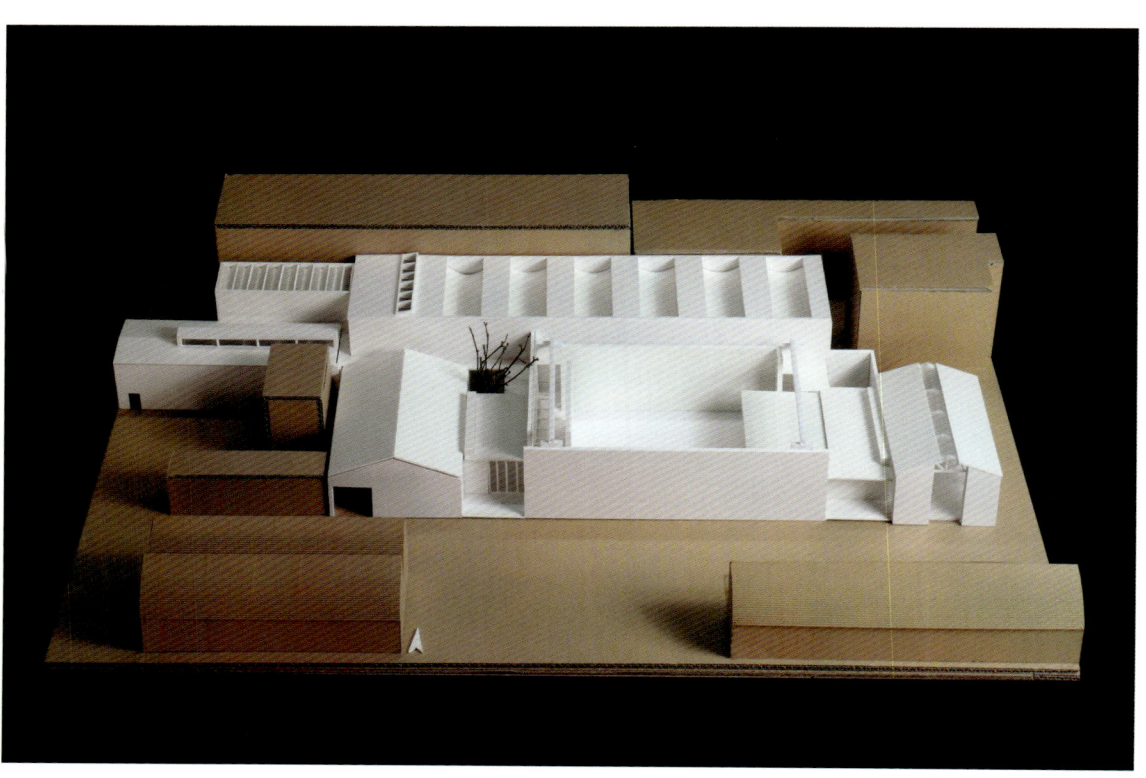

Model © Studio Zhu Pei

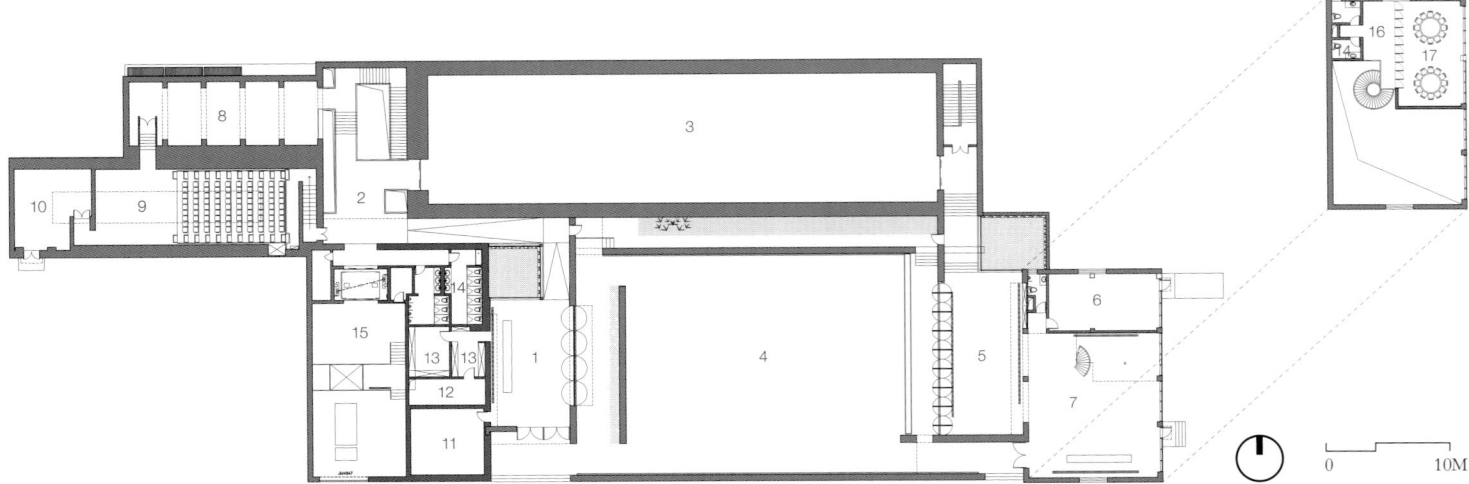

Ground-floor plan

1. Foyer
2. Lobby
3. Main exhibition area
4. Courtyard
5. Art retail center
6. Kitchen
7. Restaurant
8. Children's art education
9. Exhibition space/lecture hall
10. Storage
11. Office
12. Mechanical room
13. Coat check
14. Restrooms
15. Unloading and storage
16. Corridor
17. Private room

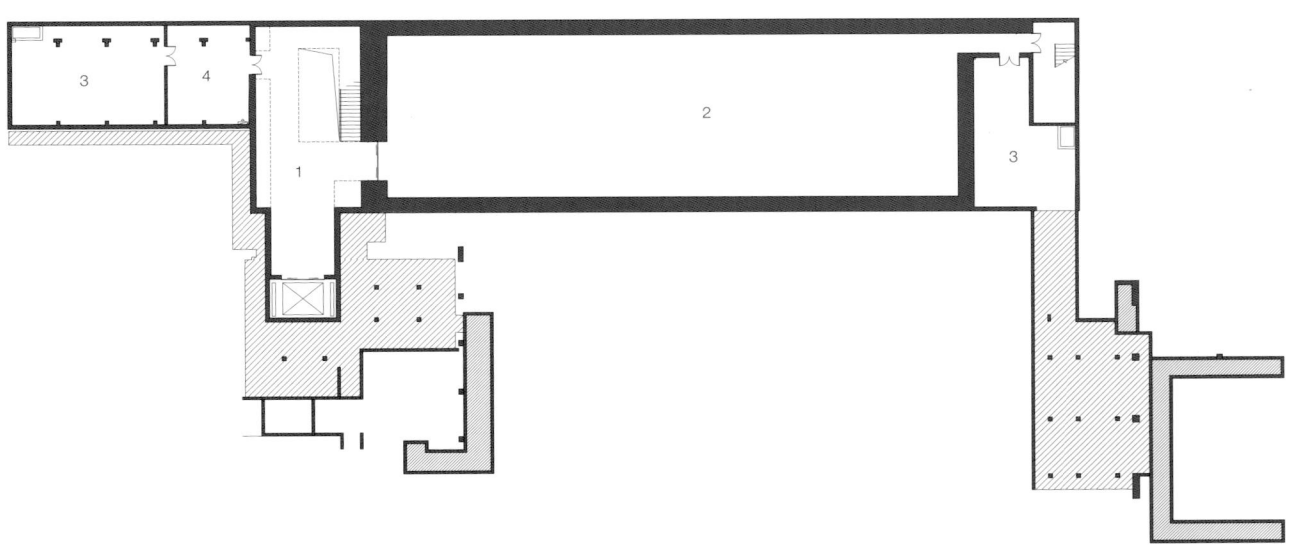

Belowground floor plan

1. Lobby
2. Main exhibition area
3. Mechanical room
4. Tool room

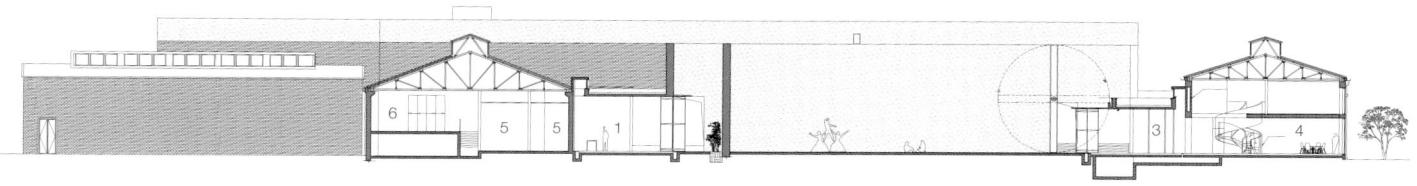

Section A

1. Foyer
2. Courtyard
3. Art retail center
4. Restaurant
5. Coat check
6. Storage and unloading

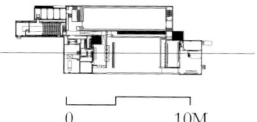

0   10M

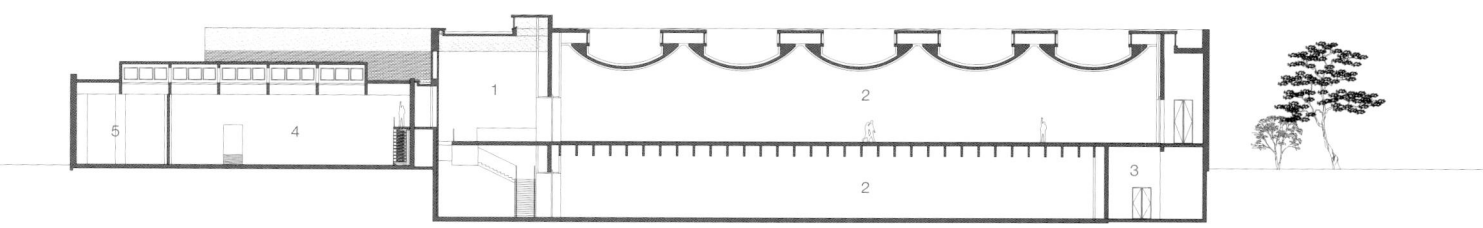

Section B

1. Lobby
2. Main exhibition area
3. Mechanical room
4. Children's art education
5. Monitoring room

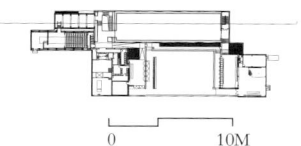

0   10M

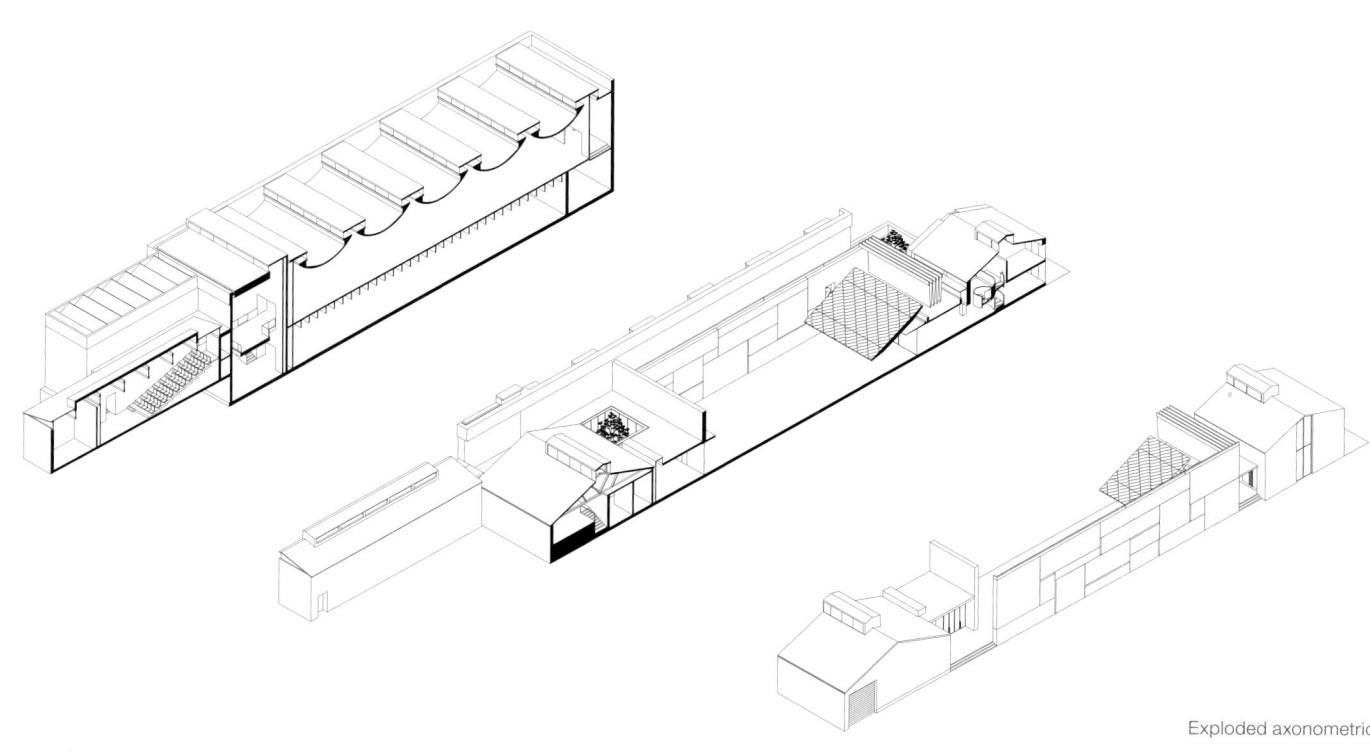

Exploded axonometric

Summer 2025   119

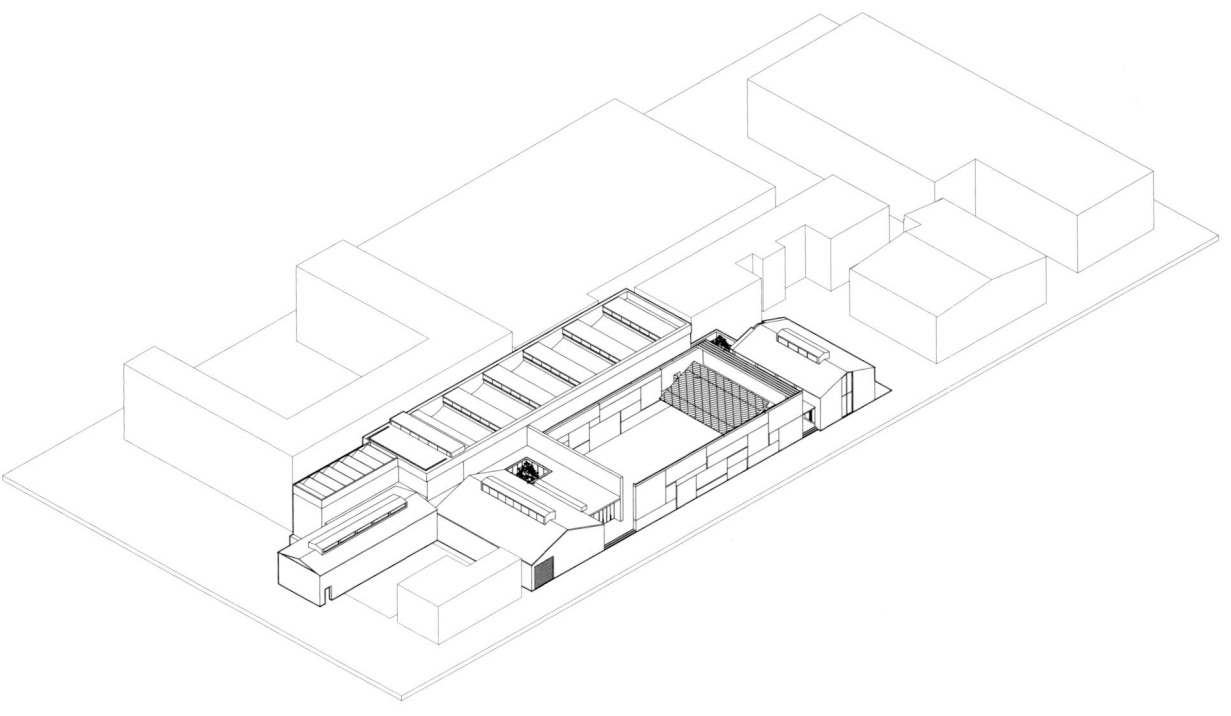

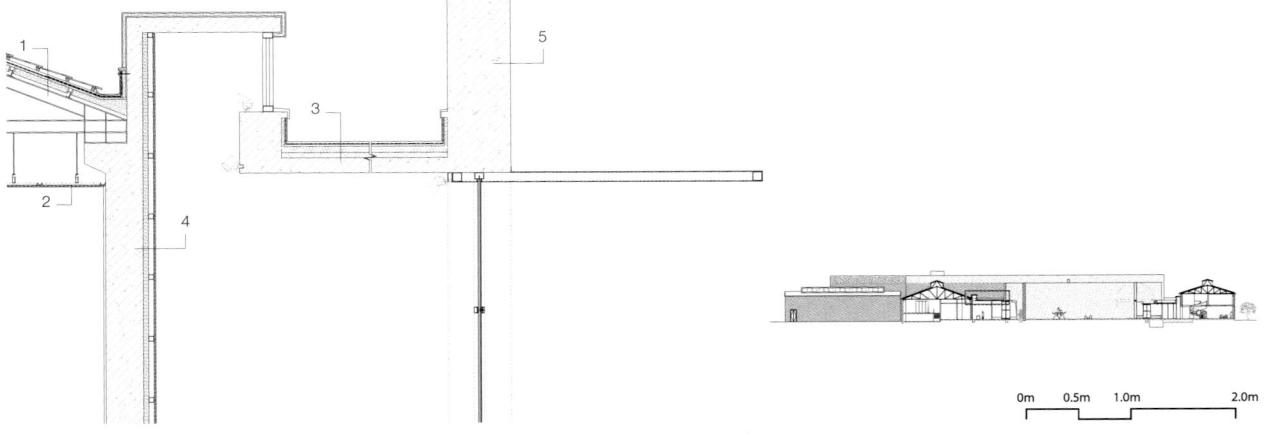

Construction system detail
Vertical section—scale 1:20

1. Gray cement pantile
   Wooden battens 30x30 mm (H)
   Wooden counter battens 30x30 mm (H) @500
   PE/PP waterproofing membrane (0.7+1.3 mm) with double layers of adhesive paste
   Plank sheathing (20 mm)
   Extruded polystyrene thermal insulation (60 mm)
   Supporting net
   Steel-wood composite purlin

2. 90x40 mm C-section aluminum profile with suspension tie rod
   Fire-resistant sheet (12 mm)
   Moisture-resistant paper-backed plasterboard (12 mm)
   White exterior wall coating

3. 1:3 cement mortar surface course (20 mm)
   PE/PP waterproofing membrane (0.7+1.3 mm) with double layers of adhesive paste
   1:3 cement mortar screed coat (20 mm)
   Extruded polystyrene thermal insulation (60 mm)
   2% slope of LC5.0 lightweight aggregate concrete sloping layer (thicker than 30 mm)
   Fair-faced concrete roof slab

4. White exterior wall coating
   Paper-backed plasterboard (12 mm)
   Fire-resistant sheet (12 mm)
   40x40x4 mm horizontal square hollow section steel
   Sound insulation mineral wool (50 mm)
   40x40x4mm vertical square hollow section steel
   Reinforced-concrete wall

5. Fair-faced concrete wall

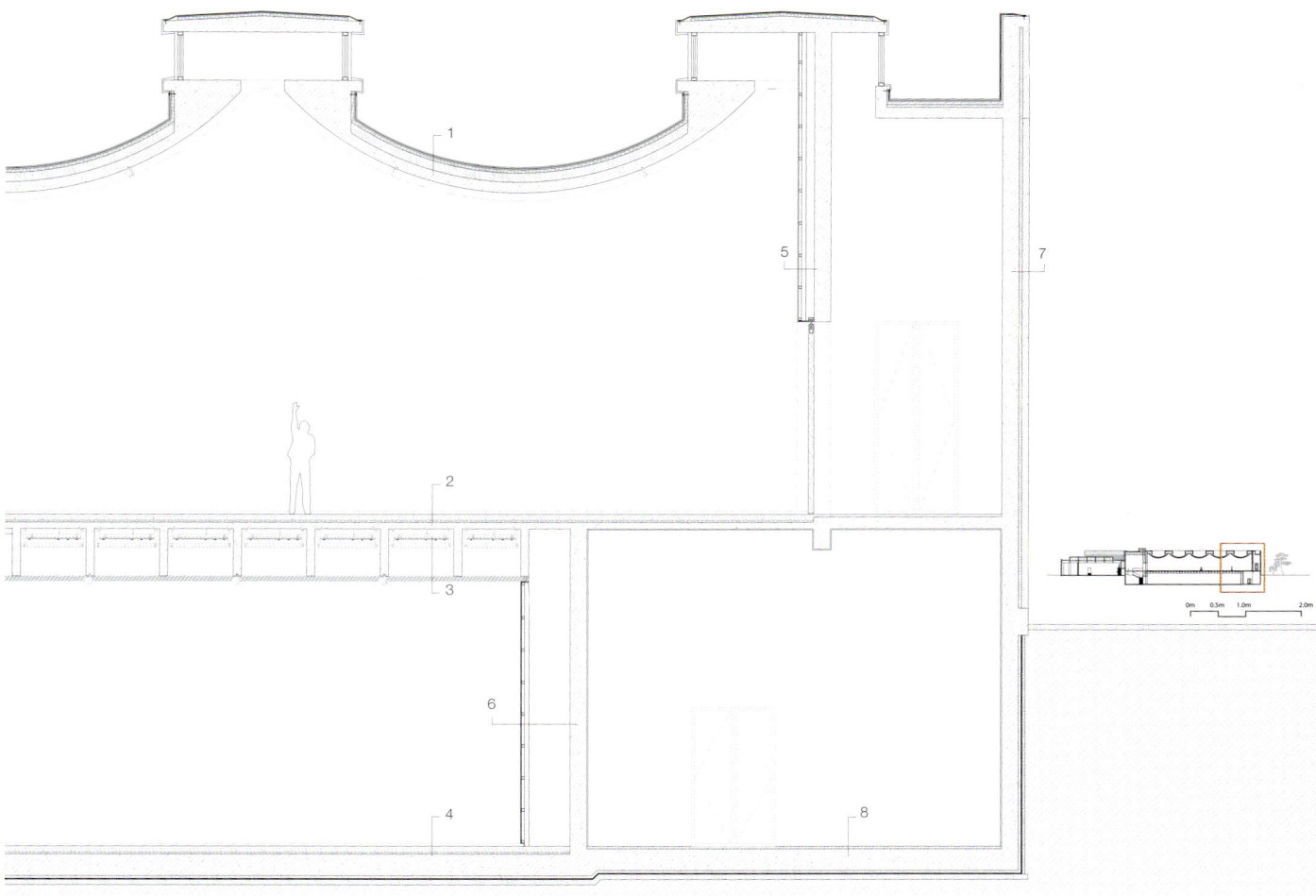

Construction system detail
Vertical section 2—scale 1:20

1. 1:3 cement mortar surface course (20 mm)
   PE/PP waterproofing membrane (0.7+1.3 mm) with double layers of adhesive paste
   1:3 cement screed coat (20 mm)
   Extruded polystyrene thermal insulation (60 mm)
   2% slope of LC5.0 lightweight aggregate concrete sloping layer (thicker than 30 mm)
   Reinforced concrete roof slab

2. Carborundum sheathing, division joint 6x6 m (50 mm)
   Fine aggregate concrete floor heating layer (equipped with Φ3 mm @50 steel wire mesh on the upper and lower, and heat pipe in the middle; 60 mm)
   Biaxially oriented polyethylene terephthalate (BOPET; 0.2 mm)
   Expanded polystyrene foam board (20 mm)
   Polyurethane coatings damp-proof course (1.5 mm)
   1:3 cement screed coat (20 mm)
   Reinforced-concrete slab

3. 90x40 mm C-section aluminum profile with suspension tie rod
   Fire-resistant sheet (12 mm)
   Moisture-resistant paper-backed plasterboard (12 mm)
   White exterior wall coating
   LED light strip
   White soft film ceiling

4. Carborundum sheathing, division joint 6x6 m (50 mm)
   Fine aggregate concrete floor heating layer (equipped with Φ3 mm @50 steel wire mesh on the upper and lower, and heat pipe in the middle; 60 mm)
   Biaxially oriented polyethylene terephthalate (BOPET; 0.2 mm)
   Expanded polystyrene foam board (20 mm)
   Polyurethane coatings damp-proof course (1.5 mm)
   1:3 cement screed coat (20 mm)
   Impermeable reinforced-concrete floor, impermeability grade P6
   DS cement mortar screed coat (20 mm)
   Primary treatment agent
   SBS polyester reinforcement modified Bitumen membrane (4+3 mm)
   EPS waterproof layer (50 mm)
   Concrete cushion (100 mm)
   Plain soil tamping

5. White exterior wall coating
   Paper-backed plasterboard (12 mm)
   Fire resistant sheet (12 mm)
   Horizontal square hollow section steel (40x40x4 mm)
   Vertical square hollow section steel (40x40x4 mm)
   Reinforced-concrete wall

6. White exterior wall coating
   Paper-backed plasterboard (12 mm)
   Fire-resistant sheet (12 mm)
   Horizontal square hollow section steel (40x40x4 mm)
   Vertical square hollow section steel (40x40x4 mm)
   Air-conditioning equipment interlayer
   Reinforced-concrete wall

7. Fair-faced concrete wall
   Extruded polystyrene board insulation layer (60 mm)
   Secondary pouring of fair-faced concrete wall

8. 1:2.5 cement mortar (15 mm)
   C15 fine aggregate concrete (35 mm)
   Polyurethane coating waterproof layer (1.5 mm)
   1:3 cement mortar screed coat (thicker than 30 mm)
   Impermeable reinforced-concrete floor, impermeability grade P6
   DS cement mortar screed coat (20 mm)
   Primary treatment agent
   SBS modified asphalt polyester tire waterproof membrane (4+3 mm)
   EPS waterproof layer (50 mm)
   Concrete cushion (100 mm)
   Plain soil tamping

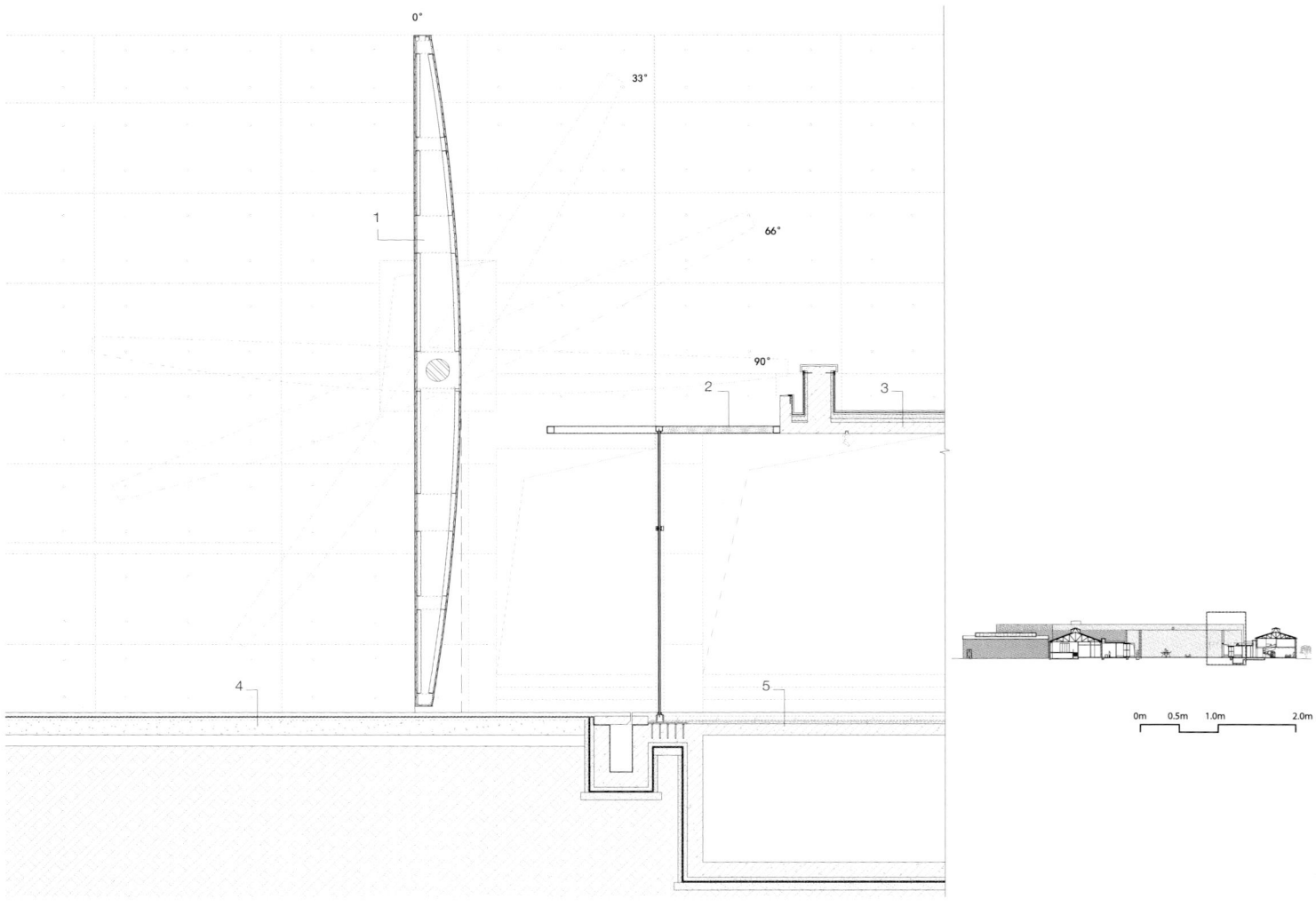

Construction system detail
Vertical section 3—scale 1:20

1. Aluminum-magnesium-manganese decorative panel (0.7 mm)
   Galvanized steel sheet (1 mm)
   SBS waterproofing membrane (2 mm)
   Profiled steel plate (0.5 mm)
   Square hollow section steel (60x60x4 mm)
   H-beam (505x400x12x20 mm)
   Seamless round steel pipe (Φ406x16 mm)

2. Stainless-steel plate (2 mm)
   SBS waterproofing membrane (2 mm)
   Profiled steel plate (0.5 mm)
   H-beam (90x100x6x8 mm)
   Stainless-steel plate (2 mm)

3. 1:3 cement mortar surface layer (20 mm)
   PE/PP waterproofing membrane (0.7+1.3 mm) with double layers of adhesive paste
   1:3 cement mortar screed coat (20 mm)
   Extruded polystyrene board insulation layer (60 mm)
   2% slope of LC5.0 lightweight aggregate concrete sloping layer (thicker than 30 mm)
   Fair-faced concrete roof slab

4. Carborundum sheathing, division joint 6x6 m (50 mm)
   Waterproof mortar (20 mm)
   Polyurethane waterproof layer (1.5 mm) or polymer cement-based permeable crystalline
   waterproof coating (2 mm)
   1:3 cement mortar or the thinnest C20 fine aggregate concrete screed coat (30 mm)
   Cement slurry (mixed with construction glue)
   C15 concrete cushion (200 mm)
   Particle size 5–32 mm pebble (gravel) filled with M2.5 mixed mortar, vibrated and compacted or 3:7 lime soil (150 mm)
   Plain soil tamping

5. Carborundum sheathing, division joint 6x6 m (50 mm)
   Fine aggregate concrete floor heating layer (equipped with Φ3 mm @50 steel wire mesh on the upper and lower, and heat pipe in the middle; 60 mm)
   Biaxially oriented polyethylene terephthalate (BOPET; 0.2 mm)
   Expanded polystyrene foam board (20 mm)
   Polyurethane coatings, damp-proof course (1.5 mm)
   1:3 cement screed coat (20 mm)
   Reinforced concrete slab
   Equipment trench
   Reinforced-concrete slab
   DS mortar screed coat (20 mm)
   Primary treatment agent
   SBS polyester reinforcement modified Bitumen membrane (4+3 mm)
   EPS waterproof layer (50 mm)
   Concrete cushion (100 mm)
   Plain soil tamping

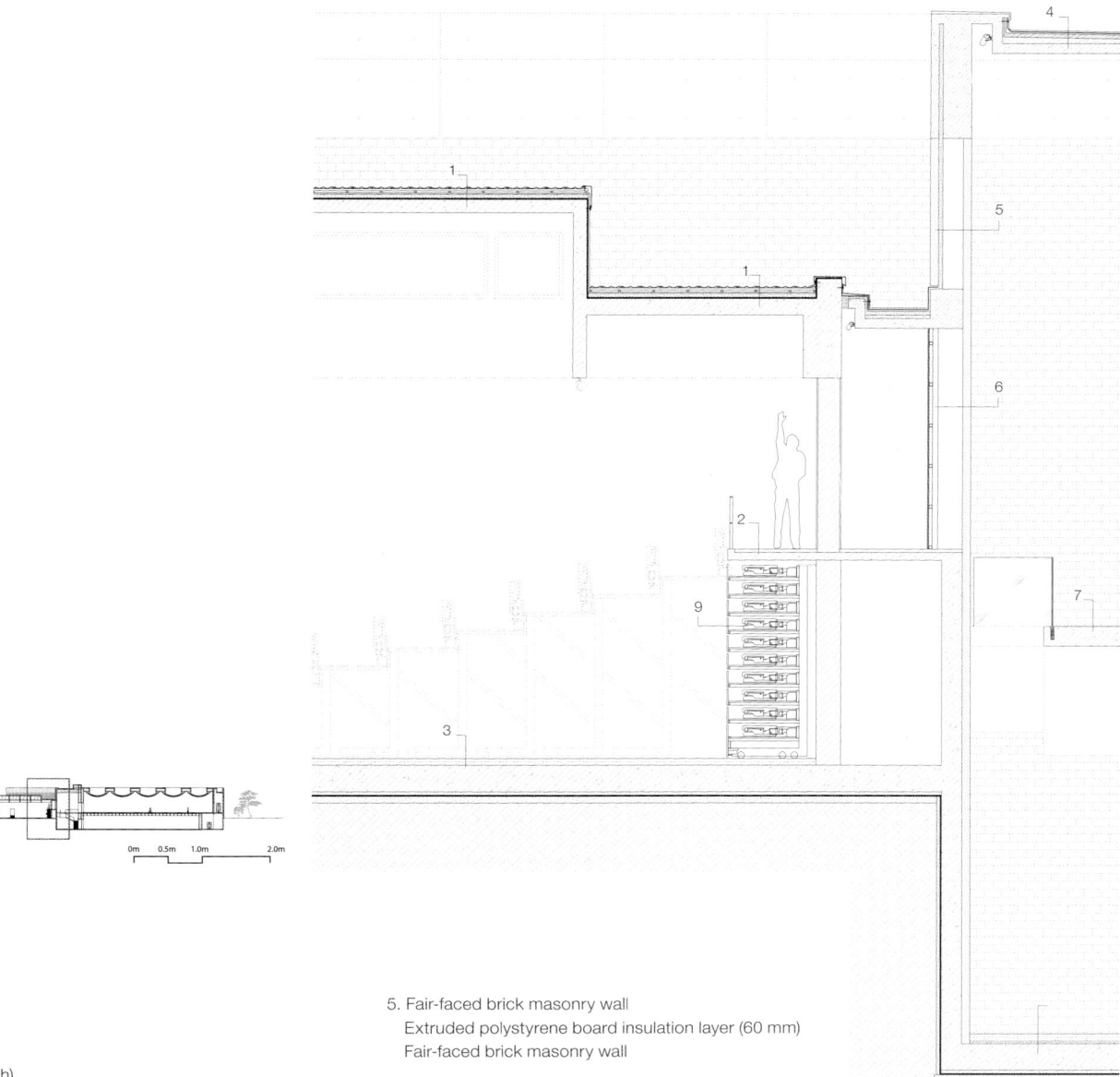

Construction system detail
Vertical section 4—scale 1:20

1. Gray cement pantile
   Wooden battens 30x30 mm (h)
   Wooden counter battens 30x30 mm (h) @500
   PE/PP waterproofing membrane (0.7+1.3 mm) with
   double layers of adhesive paste
   Plank sheathing (20 mm)
   Extruded polystyrene thermal insulation (60 mm)
   Supporting net
   Steel-wood composite purlin

2. Carborundum sheathing, division joint 6x6 m (50 mm)
   Fair-faced concrete floor

3. Carborundum sheathing, division joint 6x6m (50 mm)
   Fine aggregate concrete cushion (50 mm)
   Impermeable reinforced-concrete floor, impermeability grade P6
   DS mortar screed coat (20 mm)
   Primary treatment agent
   SBS polyester reinforcement modified Bitumen membrane
   (4+3 mm)
   EPS waterproof layer (50 mm)
   Concrete cushion (100 mm)
   Plain soil tamping

4. 1:3 cement mortar surface layer (20 mm)
   PE/PP waterproofing membrane (0.7+1.3 mm) with
   double layers of adhesive paste
   1:3 cement mortar screed coat (20 mm)
   Extruded polystyrene board insulation layer (60 mm)
   2% slope of LC5.0 lightweight aggregate concrete sloping
   layer (thicker than 30 mm)
   Fair-faced concrete roof slab

5. Fair-faced brick masonry wall
   Extruded polystyrene board insulation layer (60 mm)
   Fair-faced brick masonry wall

6. White exterior wall coating
   Paper-backed plasterboard (12 mm)
   Fire-resistant sheet (12 mm)
   Horizontal square hollow section steel (40x40x4 mm)
   Vertical square hollow section steel (40x40x4 mm)
   Fair-faced sintered brick masonry wall

7. Fair-faced concrete floor, smoothing and calendering on top surface

8. Carborundum sheathing, dividing joint 6x6 m (50 mm)
   Fine aggregate concrete floor heating layer (equipped with Φ3 mm @50
   steel wire mesh on the upper and lower, and heat pipe in the middle; 60 mm)
   Vacuum aluminized polyester film (0.2 mm)
   Expanded polystyrene foam board (20 mm)
   Polyurethane coating, damp-proof course (1.5 mm)
   1:3 cement mortar screed coat (20 mm)
   Impermeable reinforced-concrete floor, impermeability grade P6
   DS mortar screed coat (20 mm)
   Primary treatment agent
   SBS polyester reinforcement modified Bitumen membrane (4+3 mm)
   EPS waterproof layer (50 mm)
   Concrete cushion (100 mm)
   Plain soil tamping

9. Wood veneer mechanically adjustable seat

Service Station Under Wuning Road Bridge

Zhou Wei + Zhang Bin | Atelier Z+

Location: Wuning Road Bridge, Shanghai, China
Architect: Atelier Z+
Principal architect: Zhou Wei, Zhang Bin
Project architect: Xu Yue
Project team: Zhu Xiaojun
Structure consultant: AND Office for Architecture & Structure
Wooden structure design: Shanghai SKF Construction Technology Co., Ltd.
Steel structure design: Shanghai Sanyao Construction Engineering Design Co., Ltd.
M&E consultant: Shanghai Zhisheng Architectural Decoration Design Co., Ltd.
Design general contractor: CCI Architecture Design & Consulting Co., Ltd.
Client: Shanghai Putuo District Municipal Administration Center
Construction general contractor: Shanghai Putuo Municipal Engineering Co., Ltd.
Site area: 485 square meters
Gross floor area: 238.7 square meters
Design period: November 2020–April 2021
Construction period: May 2021–July 2021
Photography: Yang Min

Site plan

The service station under the Wuning Road Bridge is one of three urban citizen service stations built as demonstration projects to connect both banks of Suzhou Creek in the Putuo District of Shanghai. This project is situated beneath the bridge opening, along West Guangfu Road, on the north bank of the Suzhou Creek. The Putuo section of Suzhou Creek features many bends, and the areas along the banks claim bragging rights as the origins of China's modern national industries. Constructed in 1956, the Wuning Road Bridge spans Suzhou Creek at the mouth of Tanjia Bend. It was originally a reinforced-concrete single-arm cantilever bridge with three openings. The middle opening crossed the river, while one of the side openings crossed West Guangfu Road to form an intersection. The bridge was first widened in 1967 based on the old piers, and underwent a major reconstruction in 2000, transforming it into a three-span steel box continuous beam bridge. In 2008, in preparation of the Shanghai World Expo 2010, it was decorated in the style of the Alexander III Bridge on the Seine River in Paris. The bridge currently features 27-meter-high ionic composite column bridgeheads on both sides of the river, which have become a symbol of urban construction reminiscent of French monuments of a specific era. The areas north of the Wuning Road Bridge remain as residential pockets, characterized by urban environments woven through a mix of different programs. The service station under the Wuning Road Bridge aims to explore creative ways in which to revitalize underused urban spaces in the context of urban regeneration.

The conditions at each site of the Suzhou Creek station were too limited and complex to establish a standardized station. Therefore, we a menu-based component approach was adopted. This allowed the design team to consider the various functional spaces that would make up the station—such as restrooms,

City Stand

Before

lounges, small exhibition halls, small gardens, and gable corridors—as relatively standard spatial components of different specifications. The assembly of these components was customized according to each site's specific conditions. Also, original environment beneath the Wuning Road Bridge was unsatisfactory and did not meet the required standard. Although traffic on West Guangfu Road passing through the bridge opening isn't usually heavy, it does result in significant noise. On top of that, the heavy traffic trundling across Wuning Road above the bridge also occasionally causes vibrations.

Night view of Wuning Bridge and the service station under the bridge

Café and City Stand

Exhibition space and restrooms

Underutilised space—often either unused or used for parking

Night view

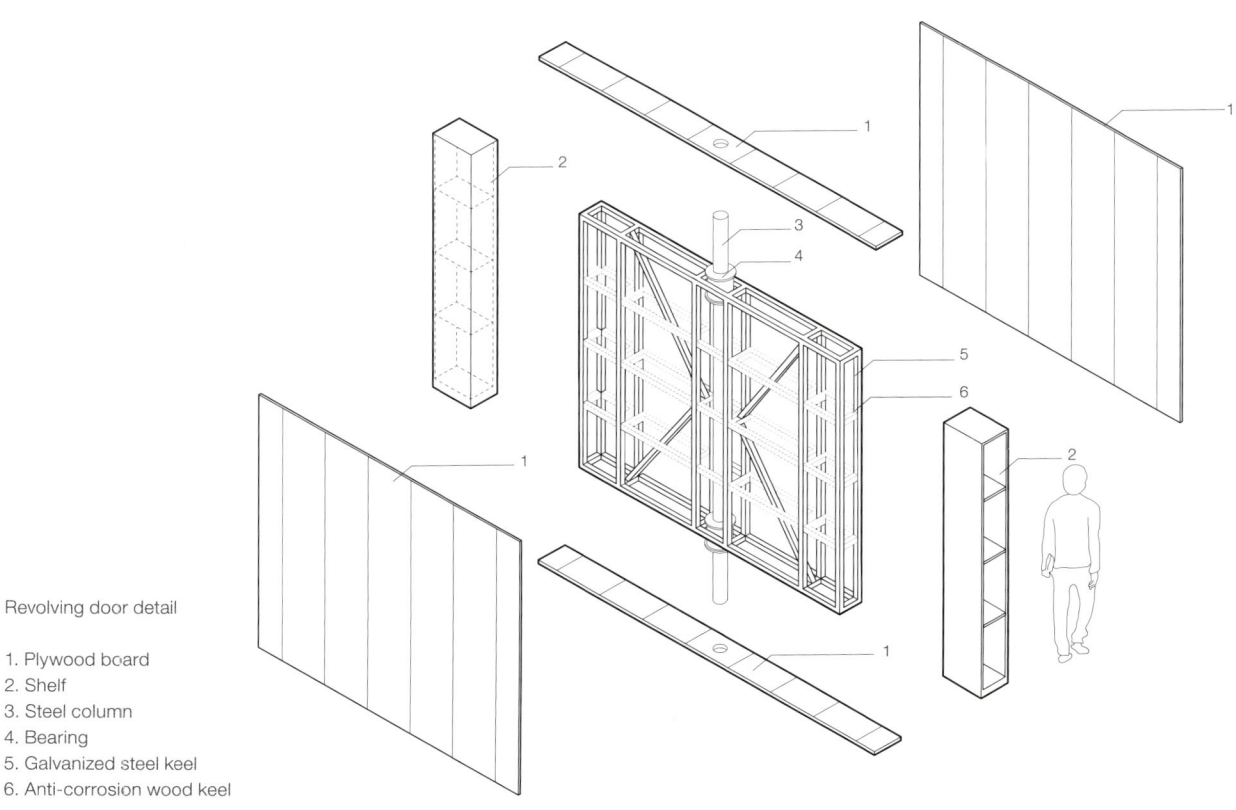

Revolving door detail

1. Plywood board
2. Shelf
3. Steel column
4. Bearing
5. Galvanized steel keel
6. Anti-corrosion wood keel

Everyday scene

Special event featuring African drums

Due to the limited space under the bridge, the service station could only be built within a narrow area measuring 2 to 3 meters in depth and 20 to 30 meters in length. Alongside essential features such as public restrooms, 24-hour service facilities, and public lounges with minimal components, the design strives to maximize space for open, flexible uses that accommodate autonomous activities. This approach is intended to create a more appealing atmosphere in an otherwise unsatisfactory environment, allowing the sounds and vibrations of passing cars to contribute to the city's ambiance. In the northern section of the service station, an open, stepped City Stand aligns with the original berm. At either end, two small rooms serve as lounges or roadside spaces, elevated slightly above the road surface and featuring seating along a timber-paved area beneath long windows. The southern section, situated near the flood prevention wall and bridge abutment, includes compact cubicle-style restrooms and service facilities such as vending machines and lockers at both ends. In the middle section, opposite the City Stand, is a miniature exhibition hall. This exhibition space features a rotating wall of doors that can be opened and closed along vertical axes, allowing for flexible displays. It defines itself as a variable stage with different opening and closing arrangements, functioning as a "theater under the bridge."

Given the limited construction conditions under the bridge, which prevented the use of large machinery, and to ensure traffic flow was unaffected, a steel-wood hybrid glued timber construction system was employed. This method allowed for the control of the scale of the structure and facilitate dsimple, rapid manual construction. The project is finished in two long, slender, warm, and bright timber volumes that have been integrated beneath a cold, gray bridge, resulting in a new, friendly, and pleasant interface between the two sides of the bridge roadway.

Shortly after the completion of the station, a café opened in the small room at the west

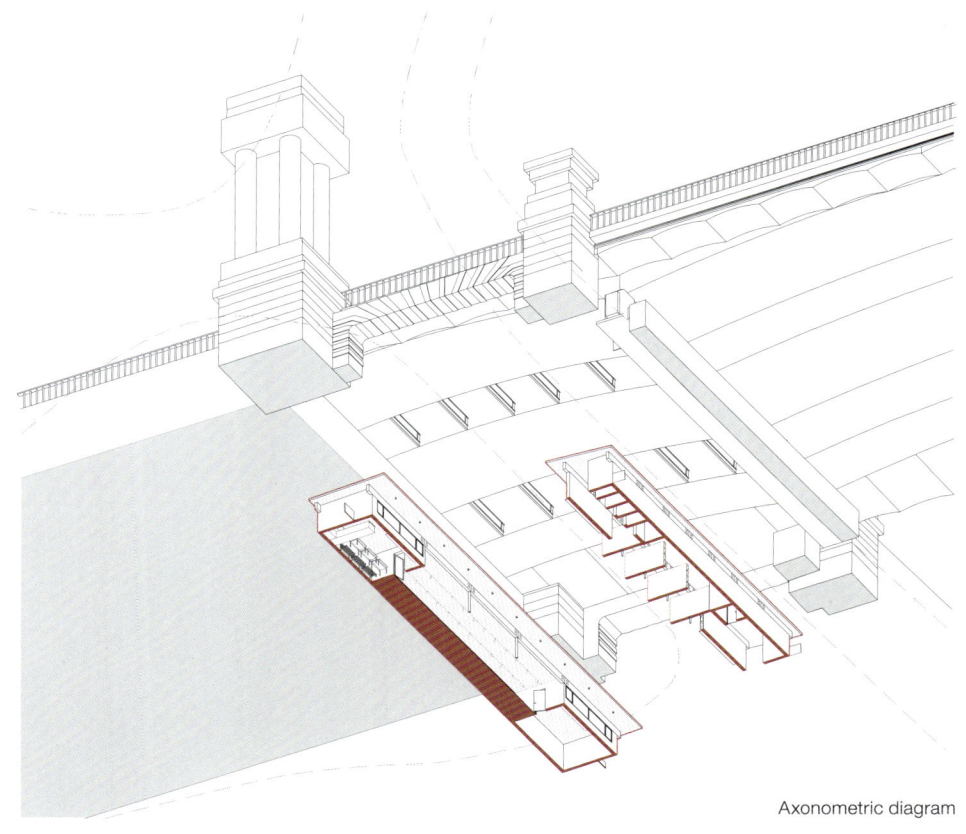

Axonometric diagram

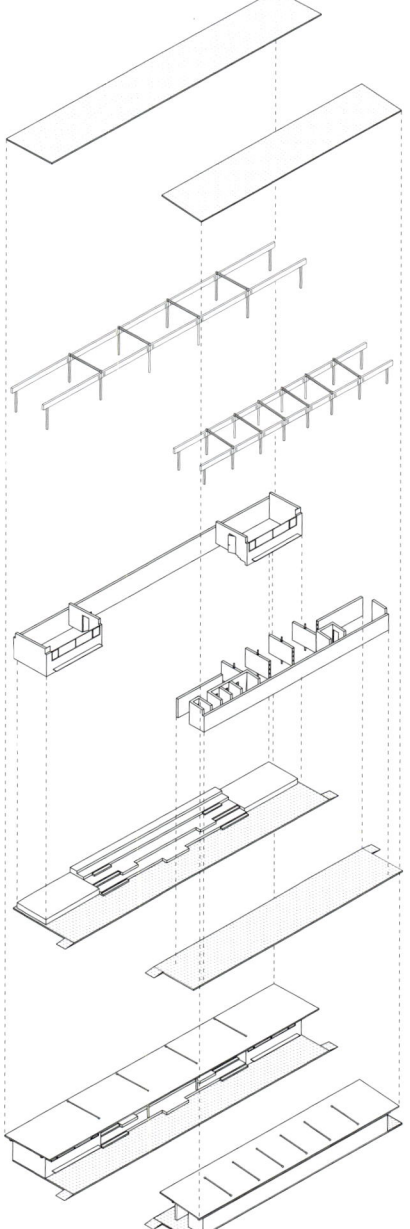

Exploded diagram

end of the City Stand. The café quickly gained popularity while operating as a non-profit establishment. This helped relieve, some pressure on the Government concerning the best use of the compact space. Over the next six months, the project attracted a diverse range of people, including local residents, young people, and foreigners. Interestingly, various urban subculture groups also "discovered" this unique venue. A month or two after the project was completed, the City Stand hosted a sharing session focused on African drums, as well as gatherings for outdoor exploration. This process of utilizing the station from its inception has allowed us to witness the vibrant energy of social diversification and community collaboration in urban life. In 2022, during the citywide COVID-19 lockdown, the station under the bridge temporarily transformed into a campsite for delivery riders, which had been essential for maintaining the city's logistics operations. At the height of the lockdown, 50 to 60 individuals stayed there on a temporary basis. The design team extends their gratitude to the owner of Café Under the Bridge for keeping the indoor and outdoor lights on even when the café was closed. In a city where resources are limited for emergencies, the Wuning Road Bridge service station was seen emerging as a vital emergency "outlet" for public space.

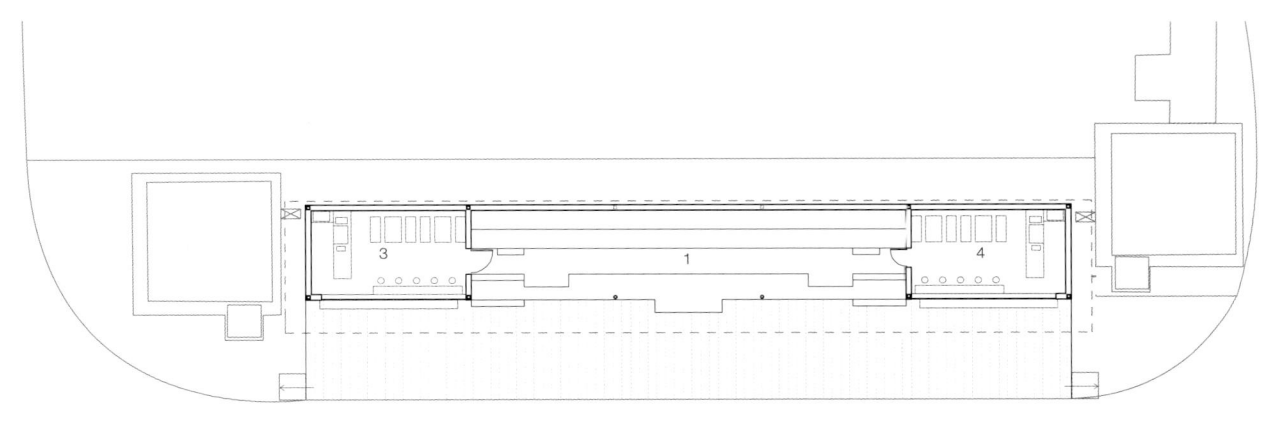
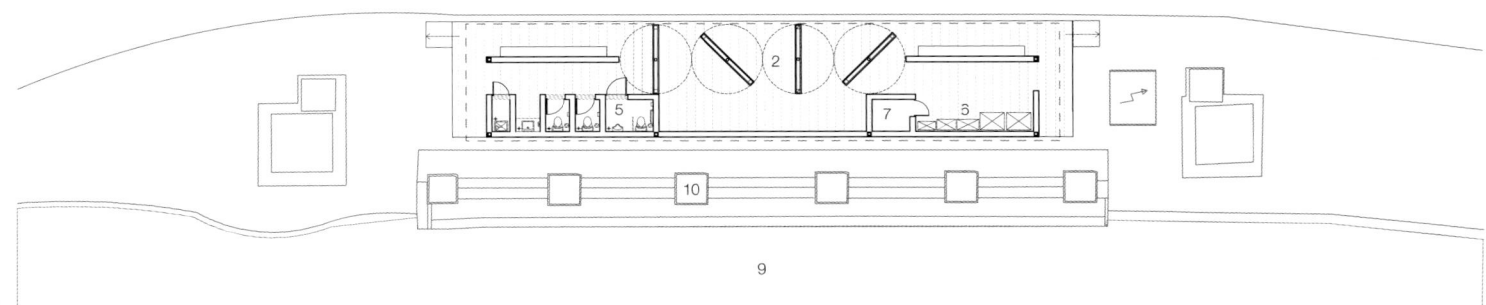

Ground floor plan

1. City Stand
2. Showroom
3. Café
4. Public lounge
5. Public restroom
6. 24-hour service facilities
7. Electricity distribution room
8. West Guangfu Road
9. Suzhou Creek
10. Pier

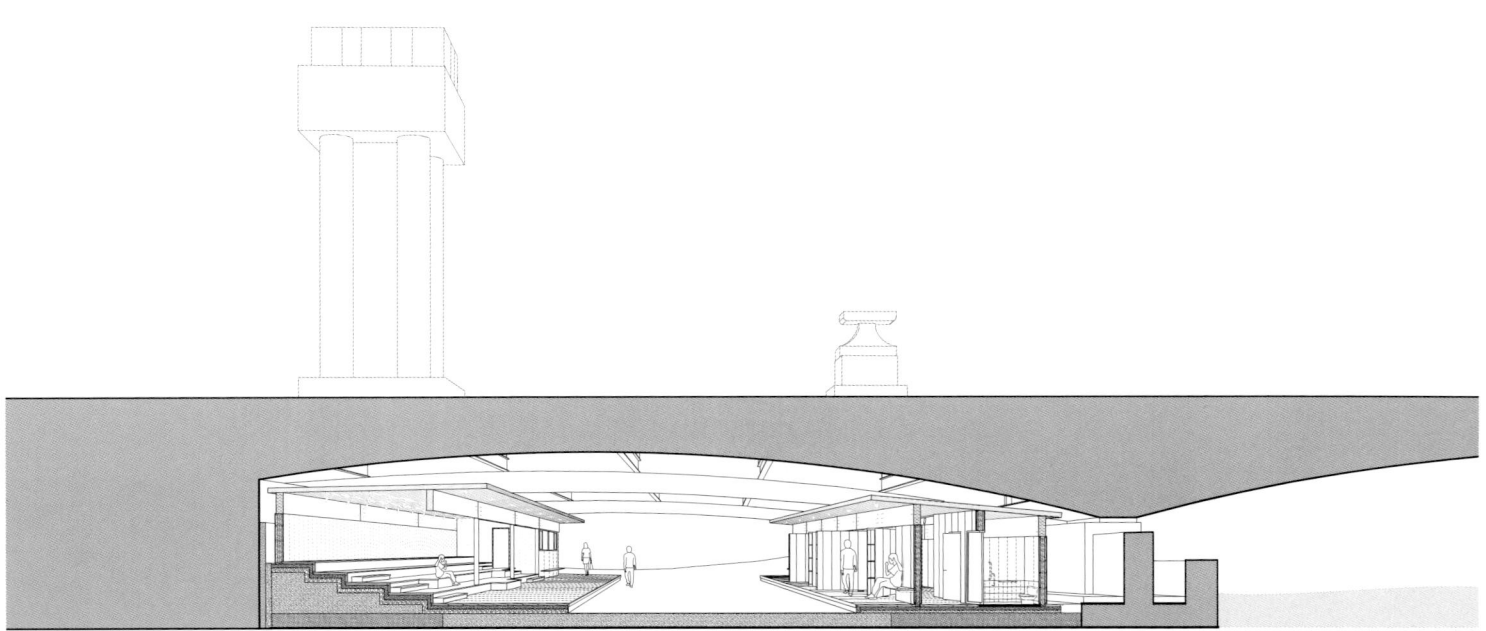

Section perspective

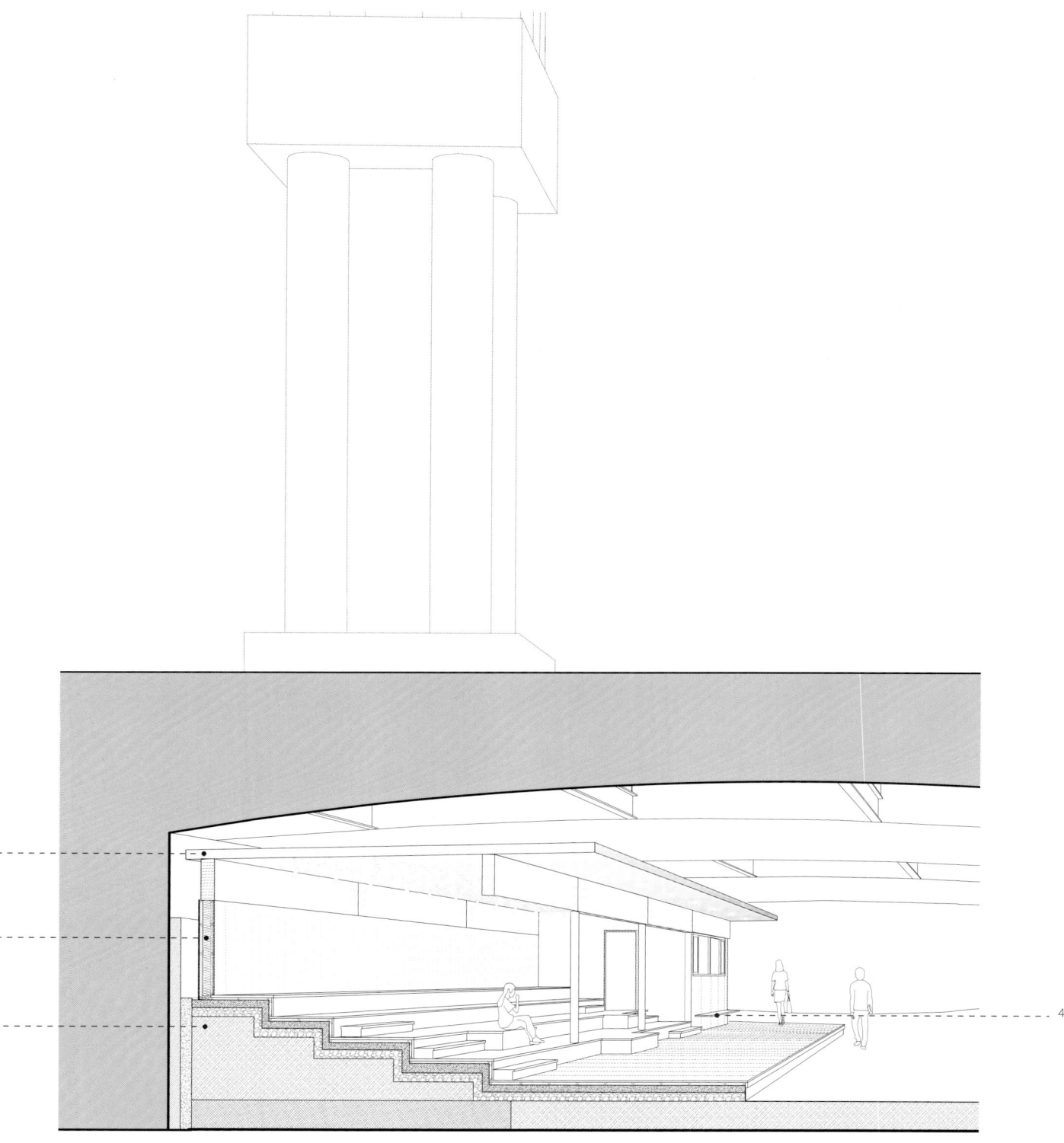

Detail

1. NLT roofing:
   400-mm-wide and 0.9-mm-thick aluminum-magnesium metal roof tile cladding
   35×145 mm NLT dense paving
   35×200 mm spruce matting
   Steel beam

2. Plywood board wall:
   300×20 mm plywood veneer
   Double-layer 45×38 mm anti-corrosive wood keel
   0.15 mm thick plastic film
   38 mm×140 mm wall studs
   9.5 mm thick OSB board
   0.15 mm thick waterproof membrane
   45×38 mm anti-corrosive wood keel
   300×20 mm plywood veneer

3. Outdoor wood deck:
   38×184 mm anti-corrosive wood decking
   38×45 mm high anti-septic wood keel
   120 mm thick C25 concrete
   150 mm thick gravel filling DM2.5 mortar
   (plain soil tamping, tamping degree ≥ 93%)

4. Wood seating
   2-195 SPF veneer
   80×60 mm T-beam

Hunan Street Integrated Service Station

Yuan Ye + Zhang Ziyue | Steam Architecture

Location: Lane 157, Wuyuan Road, Xuhui District, Shanghai, China
Architect: Steam Architecture
Principal architect: Yuan Ye + Zhang Ziyue
Program: Waste public toilet; transfer station; staff room
Local design institute: Guangzhou Southern Architectural Design & Research Institute Shanghai Branch
Client: Shanghai Xuhui District Greening and Cityscape Management Bureau
Site area: 124 square meters
Gross floor area: 190 square meters
Design and completion: 2022
Photography: Xiao Xiao, Chen Min, Steam Architecture

Site plan

In recent years, Shanghai has undergone an urban regeneration process through which existing urban space regains its vitality through spatial regeneration and institutional improvements. One notable example of this is the renovation of the Hunan Street Integrated Service Station, which represents a top-down micro renewal of public facilities. Located at the southwest corner of the intersection of Wuyuan Road and Urumqi Middle Road in Shanghai's Xuhui District, this facility serves thousands of users daily. The original structure is a curved, two-story building (partially three stories) featuring a colonnade, public restrooms, and a waste transfer station on the first floor. The second and third floors house offices and cabins for sanitation workers. However, the building's appearance and functionality had gradually become outdated and no longer met the evolving needs of the community as a space located in the city center. Therefore, a renovation and renewal had become essential in order to ensure the building's continued usefulness. In October 2020, the client initiated a call for renovation proposals, and by December 2020, the results were announced. After undergoing a preliminary selection process, public voting, and expert evaluations, the proposal submitted by Steam Architecture was chosen as the winner and selected for implementation.

Existing Condition

The existing colonnade is the most prominent visual feature of the building. However, due to the height difference between the interior and exterior, the colonnade is narrow and closed at both ends, preventing passage through it. While the renovation could not enclose this colonnade, it was not necessary to preserve it. The focus of the renovation was concentrated on the first floor of the original building, which houses the waste transfer station. This station operates independently, and the design needed to maintain its original position while maximizing its area. The entrances to the men's and women's restrooms were located on the east and west sides of the management room. The men's restroom was accessible from the street via the colonnade, while the women's restroom and a third accessible toilet were accessed through a shared patio between the building and the neighboring house to the west. This design complicated the management's ability to oversee foot traffic on both sides simultaneously. Additionally, the women's restroom was also very small, and the ratio of male to female toilet seats was disproportionate. During hours of peak

Street corner perspective © Xiao Xiao

pedestrian flow, it often resulted in long queues for the women's restroom. The entrance to the accessible third toilet was located in the patio, just outside the women's restroom, making it hard for passersby to notice it. This accessible toilet was rarely used due to its small entrance and had inadequate space for to accommodate wheelchair access. The core challenge of this renovation was to adapt the functionality of the plan while creating a public facility that fosters an urban atmosphere, so that the public could used the facility freely without feeling they were being put in a compromised state.

The building in the early morning when sanitation workers begin work © Xiao Xiao

© Steam Architecture

© Steam Architecture

© Chen Min

© Chen Min

Before renovation

© Chen Min

© Steam Architecture

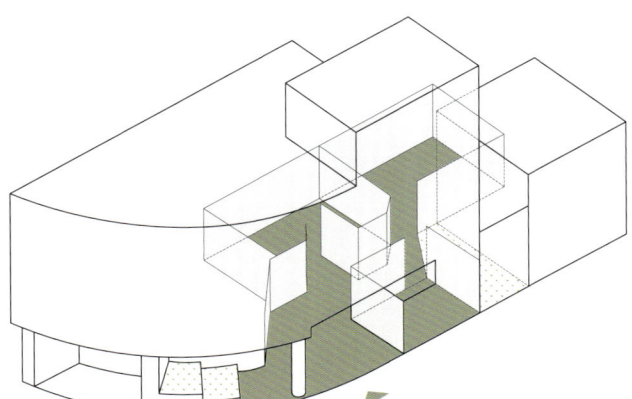
Conceptual diagram

Cave-like space as main entrance © Xiao Xiao

Design Strategy

In the competition phase, the design proposed a public circulation that connects the city street with the interior of the building, and organizes the flow of people and views through this line. This strategy presents large-scale "openings" along the street frontage of the building to create the image of a public building, while internally, the patio is transformed to act as the main landscape feature.

The design of the new building had to comply with relevant regulations for public restrooms while maintaining the same number of toilet spaces, which posed a significant challenge given the limited space available. To address this, the design integrates the sinks for both the men's and women's restrooms into a semi-outdoor public handwashing area. Additionally, a third accessible toilet has been placed in the management room of the original building, bringing it closer to the entrance and ensuring it meets regulatory requirements. The location of the women's restroom remains unchanged; however, their entry has been enhanced for a more intimate and comfortable experience through an elongated circulation pathway and landscaped courtyard. The cubicles are positioned parallel to the wall, creating a more spacious aisle for users. The courtyard serves not only as a visual feature for the public restroom but also helps delineate the urban boundary between the service station and the neighboring houses, providing an appealing landscape element for the community.

The façade of the building has also been modified in terms of material and scale to make the main entrance more visible from the street. The design slightly lowers the eaves of the ground floor to align the outside with the scale

Previous colonnade hidden by flower beds and façade structure after renovation © Xiao Xiao

of the nearby shops, while the eaves at the entrance on the first floor are raised to create a larger opening. Alongside this design choice, the perception of the entrance is enhanced through the use of floor-to-ceiling windows and green tiles on the first-floor office façade. To create a smoother flow of movement into and out of the building, the visual character of the original frame colonnade has been subdued using various design elements such as folded panel molding, green tiles, and flower beds. Only the slightly decorative columns at the entrance have been retained. While the façade has not undergone radical changes, it has been subtly transformed to reflect the character of a new building. The movement of the planes, within the constraints of the structure and equipment, along with the façade design, ensures that the public circulation originally intended can function effectively.

This design takes influence from the architect's daily experiences of urban life in Shanghai, where the sight of flowers emerging from walls often brings joy. This initial inspiration led to a series of decisions regarding the use of spatial resources, as well as the selection of forms, scales, and materials. The desire for a "corner garden" serves as a starting point for the design; however, the complex relationships that develop during the building's construction ultimately surpass the personal preferences of the architects.

Streets, flower beds, and mirrored courtyards © Xiao Xiao

Project Implementation

During the implementation phase, the design faced challenges both from the scheme itself and from external factors. This situation prompted the architects to continually reassess their initial judgments and refine the design, ultimately achieving a more balanced state filled with realistic tension. Throughout this process, they gained valuable experience from the field.

The first challenge involved the drawings required for the design work. The client was unable to provide complete drawings for the building, largely due to its age and the multiple renovations it had undergone over the years. As the conceptual design relied on preliminary drawings from structural inspections, it was challenging to match the dimensions in the later design phase to the actual site. Given the tight dimensions of the plan, any overlapping errors would easily compromise the validity of the design strategy, requiring repeated checks. The second challenge hit the team from a less technical aspect and was more about maintaining a friendly relationship with the surrounding neighborhood. On-site, the architects worked hard to engage with residents who approached them, taking their valuable suggestions into account. Top-down micro-renewal projects require respect for residents' opinions regarding the building's design; however, there is no formal mechanism to ensure that these opinions are expressed. Consequently, the viewpoints of nearby residents became essential insights that enabled architects to consider all aspects of urban life. Addressing management challenges is equally important, as these usually take root at the core of the contradictions found in urban micro-regeneration projects. The building operator wanted to completely enclose the entire structure during non-operational hours, but the alterations needed for this would undermine nearly all prior efforts. After extensive negotiations, the architects decided to install a discreet roller shutter in the corridor. When closed, this shutter left the public washbasins and flowerbeds visible. However, after the project was completed, Shanghai quickly adopted a 24-hour operation policy, making the roller shutter a relic of outdated urban governance.

1 / 2

1. Public movement from the street to the courtyard © Xiao Xiao
2. Spatial relationship of the service station, courtyard, and neighboring buildings © Xiao Xiao

Concluding Remarks

The architect not only sought a design experience but was also deeply concerned about how the selection mechanism for design schemes would affect the future of a city's public facilities. The successful progress of this project can be attributed to the fact that the preliminary scheme was subjected the rigors of competition, and it also underwent professional evaluation. Because of that the client showed a willingness to trust and support for the scheme when decisions were made. This selection mechanism has proven to be more effective than the usual approach of architects having to persuade the client to trust their vision. It also helps eliminate unpredictable changes during the implementation phases.

1. Shared handwashing area for both the male and female restrooms © Xiao Xiao
2. Courtyard and roof allowing for skylight and ventilation © Xiao Xiao

1. Entrance to male and female restrooms from the courtyard © Xiao Xiao
2. Tile and paint details © Xiao Xiao
3. Staff room © Xiao Xiao

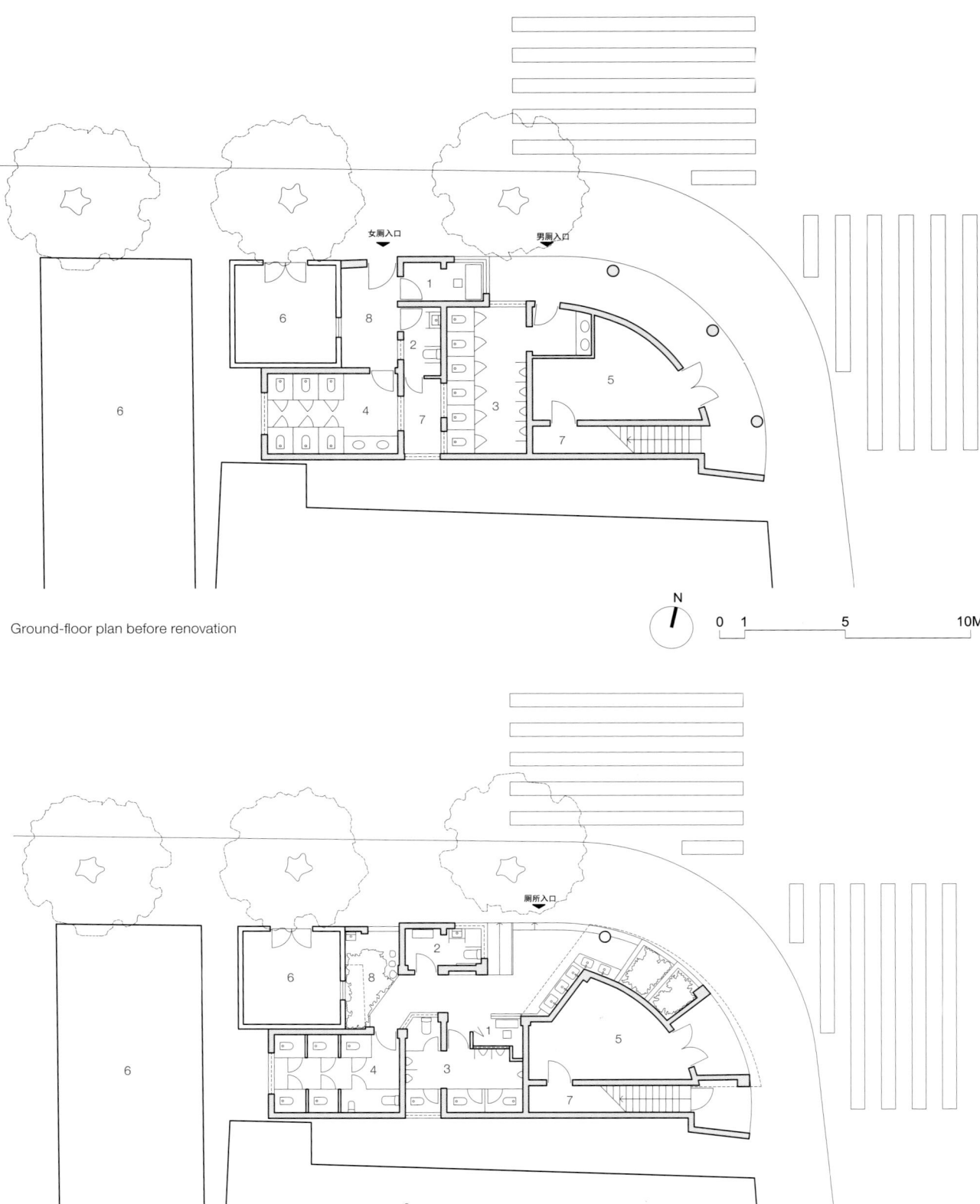

Ground-floor plan before renovation

Ground-floor plan after renovation

1. Management room
2. Accessible toilet
3. Men's restroom
4. Women's restroom
5. Refuse transfer station
6. Neighboring buildings
7. Storage
8. Coutyard

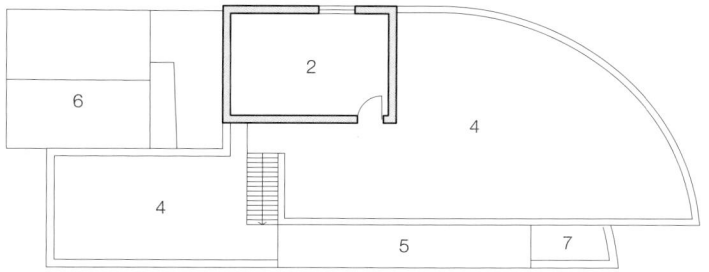

Third-floor plan

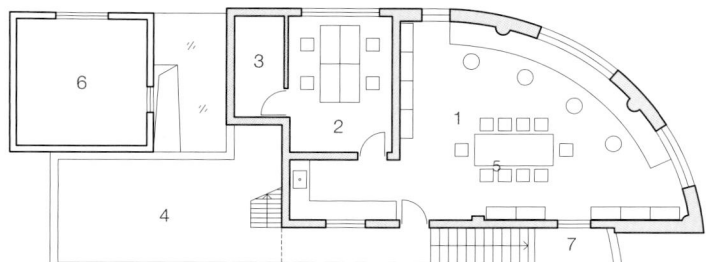

Second-floor plan

1. Staff room
2. Office
3. Storage
4. Rooftop
5. Existing rain-shelter canopy
6. Neighboring buildings
7. Mechanical platform

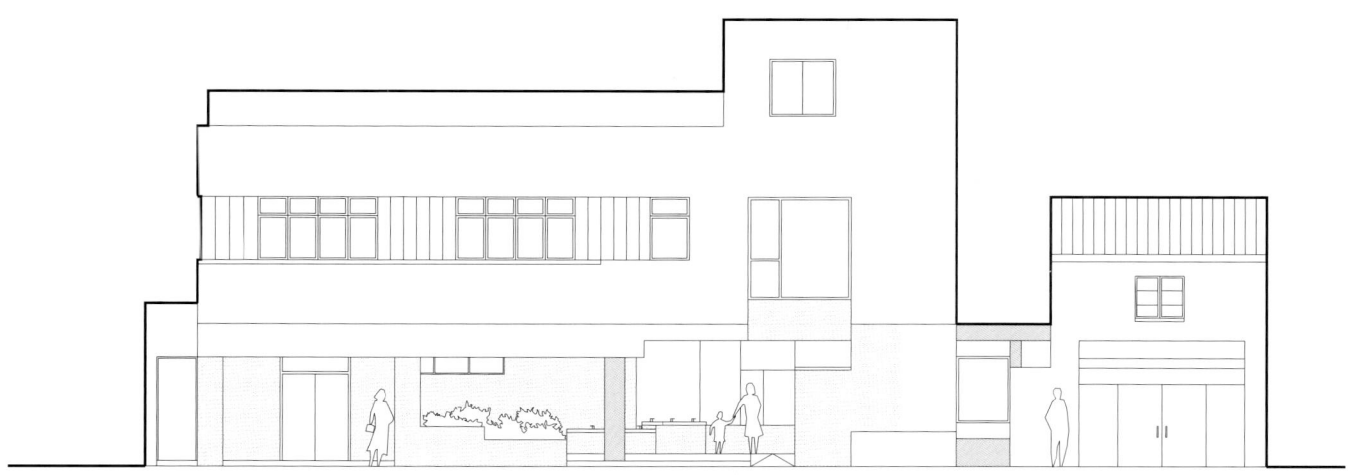

Street façade

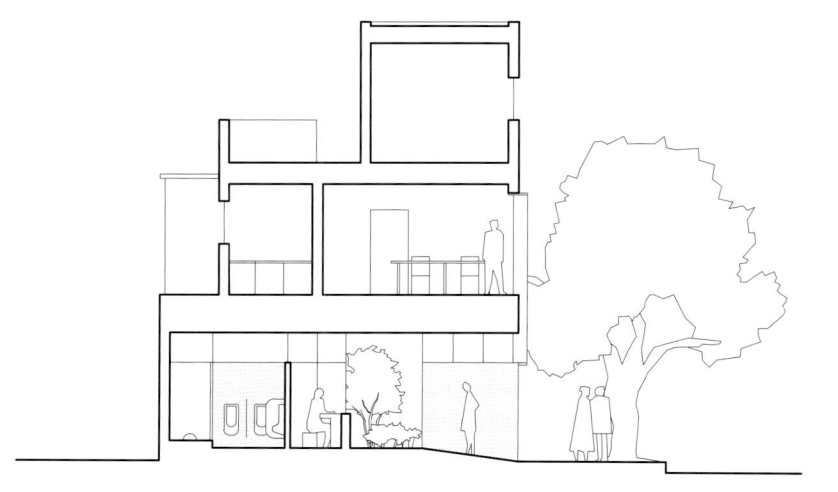

Section

Summer 2025 **141**

Liu Jiakun Receives the 2025 Pritzker Architecture Prize

The Pritzker Architecture Prize announces Liu Jiakun, of Chengdu, People's Republic of China, as the 2025 Laureate of the Pritzker Architecture Prize. This award is regarded internationally as architecture's highest honor.

"Architecture should reveal something—it should abstract, distill and make visible the inherent qualities of local people. It has the power to shape human behavior and create atmospheres, offering a sense of serenity and poetry, evoking compassion and mercy, and cultivating a sense of shared community," expresses Liu.

Intertwining seeming antipodes such as "utopia versus everyday existence," "history versus modernity," and collectivism versus individuality, Liu offers affirming architecture that celebrates the lives of ordinary citizens. He upholds the transcendent power of the built environment through the harmonizing of cultural, historical, emotional, and social dimensions, using architecture to forge community, inspire compassion, and elevate the human spirit.

"Through an outstanding body of work of deep coherence and constant quality, Liu Jiakun imagines and constructs new worlds, free from any aesthetic or stylistic constraint. Instead of a style, he has developed a strategy that never relies on a recurring method but rather on evaluating the specific characteristics and requirements of each project differently. That is to say, Liu Jiakun takes present realities and handles them to the point of offering sometimes a whole new scenario of daily life. Beyond knowledge and techniques, common sense and wisdom are the most powerful tools he adds to the designer's toolbox." — excerpt from 2025 Jury Citation

Liu creates public areas in populated cities where the luxury of space is largely absent, forging a positive relationship between density and open space. By multiplying typologies within one project, he innovates the role of civic spaces to support the breadth of requisites for a diverse society. West Village (Chengdu, China, 2015) is a five-story project that spans an entire block, visually and contextually contrasting with the matrix of characteristically mid- and high-rise buildings. An open yet enclosed perimeter of sloping pathways for cyclists and pedestrians envelopes a vibrant city of cultural, athletic, recreational, and business activities within while allowing the public to view through to the surrounding natural and built environments. The Department of Sculpture at Sichuan Fine Arts Institute (Chongqing, China, 2004) displays an alternate solution to maximizing space, with upper levels protruding outward to extend the square footage of a narrow footprint.

"Cities tend to segregate functions, but Liu Jiakun takes the opposite approach and sustains a delicate balance to integrate all dimensions of the urban life," comments Alejandro Aravena, Chair of the Jury and 2016 Pritzker Prize Laureate. He continues, "In a world that tends to create endless dull peripheries, he has found a way to build places that are a building, infrastructure, landscape, and public space all at the same time. His work may offer impactful clues on how to confront the challenges of urbanization, in an era of rapidly growing cities."

Throughout his works, Liu demonstrates a reverence for culture, history, and nature, chronicling time and comforting users with familiarity through modern interpretations of classic Chinese architecture. Flat eaves of the Suzhou Museum of Imperial Kiln Brick (Suzhou, China, 2016) and window walls of Lancui Pavilion of Egret Gulf Wetland (Chengdu, China 2013) reimagine the form of pavilions dating back many millennia. The tiered balconies of Novartis (Shanghai) Block C6 (Shanghai, China, 2014) are reminiscent of towers represented in many dynasties. Luyeyuan Stone Sculpture Art Museum (Chengdu, China, 2002), housing Buddhist sculptures and relics, is modeled after a traditional Chinese garden, balancing water and ancient stones to reflect the natural landscape. Believing that the human relationship with nature is reciprocal, buildings both emerge and dissolve within their surroundings, such as The Renovation of Tianbao Cave District of Erlang Town (Luzhou, China, 2021) nestled in the lush cliffside landscape of Tianbao Mountain. Local and wild flora is featured in all of his works. Bricks are paved upended so grass can flourish flourish through their cores; groves of bamboo, indigenous to the land, are planted in new sites; and floors and ceilings are designed with openings to allow the continuance of existing trees.

His honest architecture presents the sincerity of textural materials and processes, displaying imperfections that endure, rather than degrade, through time. He disfavors manufactured product, preferring traditional craft, often using raw local materials that sustain the economy and environment, built for and by the community. The Department of Sculpture building exposes swirling details of authentic Chongqing sand plastering handiwork that are left visible rather than honed. He revives materials—and spirits—upcycling rubble from the ruins of the 2008 Wenchuan earthquake and strengthening it with local wheat fiber and cement to produce fortified bricks with greater physical and economic efficiency than the original. These "RebirthBricks" can be found extensively throughout the Novartis building, Shuijingfang Museum (Chengdu, China, 2013) and West Village, his largest work. The devastation also yielded his smallest work to date, the Hu Huishan Memorial (Chengdu, China, 2009), a permanent cement "relief tent," exhibited not only to memorialize a 15-year-old girl who was a victim of the earthquake, but also for the collective memory of an entire nation in mourning.

"Liu Jiakun uplifts through the process and purpose of architecture, fostering emotional connections that unite communities," remarks Tom Pritzker, Chairman of The Hyatt Foundation, which sponsors the Pritzker Architecture Awards. "There is a wisdom in his architecture, philosophically looking beyond the surface to reveal that history, materials, and nature are symbiotic."

West Village, 2015 © Chen Chen

The Renovation of Tianbao Cave District of Erlang Town, 2021 © Arch-Exist

NEWS

Liu's career spans over four decades, with more than thirty projects ranging from academic and cultural institutions to civic spaces, commercial buildings, and urban planning throughout China. Significant works also include Museum of Clocks, Jianchuan Museum Cluster (Chengdu, China, 2007); The Department of Sculpture at Sichuan Fine Arts Institute (Chongqing, China, 2006), Lodging Center of China International Practice Exhibition of Architecture (Nanjing, China, 2012), Chengdu High-Tech Zone Tianfu Software Park Communication Center (Chengdu, China, 2010), and Songyang Culture Neighborhood (Lishui, China, 2020).

Liu is the 54th Laureate of the Pritzker Architecture Prize and the founder of Jiakun Architecture, established in 1999. Born in Chengdu, China, he resides and works in his native city. He will be honored at a celebration in Abu Dhabi, United Arab Emirates this spring, and globally with a virtual ceremony video this fall. The 2025 Laureate Lecture and Panel Discussion will be held in May and open to the public in-person and online.

About the Pritzker Architecture Prize
The Pritzker Architecture Prize was founded in 1979 by the late Jay A. Pritzker and his wife, Cindy. Its purpose is to honor each year a living architect or architects whose built work demonstrates a combination of the qualities of talent, vision, and commitment, which has produced consistent and significant contributions to humanity and the built environment through the art of architecture.

Songyang Culture Neighborhood, 2020 © Arch-Exist

Jury Citation
The Pritzker Architecture Prize is conferred in acknowledgment of those qualities of talent, vision, and commitment, which have persistently produced significant contributions to humanity and the built environment through the art of architecture.

In a global context where architecture is struggling to find adequate responses to fast evolving social and environmental challenges, Liu Jiakun has provided convincing answers that also celebrate the everyday lives of people as well as their communal and spiritual identities.

Through an outstanding body of work of deep coherence and constant quality, Liu Jiakun imagines and constructs new worlds, free from any aesthetic or stylistic constraint. Instead of a style, he has developed a strategy that never relies on a recurring method but rather on evaluating the specific characteristics and requirements of each project differently. That

Novartis (Shanghai) Block C6, 2014 © Arch-Exist

Suzhou Museum of Imperial Kiln Brick, 2016 © Jiakun Architecture

NEWS

is to say, Liu Jiakun takes present realities and handles them to the point of offering a whole new scenario of daily life. Beyond knowledge and technique, he adds common sense and wisdom to the designer's toolbox.

The built environment is often being pulled in opposite directions. While density appears to be a more sustainable solution for people to live together, the scarcity of space usually implies a poor quality of life. Liu Jiakun rethinks the fundamentals of density through cohabitation, crafting an intelligent solution that balances the opposite forces at play. Through transformative projects like West Village in Chengdu, he reshapes the paradigm of public spaces and of community life. He invents new, independent, shared ways of living together in which density does not represent the opposite of an open system. He also enables adaptation, expansion, and replicability. Liu Jiakun enhances and welcomes the life that inhabitants bring to his projects, creating an architecture activated by its publics.

In Liu Jiakun's work, identity is as much about the individual as it is about the collective sense of belonging to a place. He revisits the Chinese tradition as a springboard for innovation, devoid of nostalgia or ambiguity. For him, identity refers to a country's history, the traces of its cities, and the relics of its communities. At the same time, he integrates the local and global dimensions with unprecedented results. In his subtle, memorable museums, the Suzhou Museum of Imperial Kiln Brick or the Shuijingfang Museum in Chengdu, he creates new architecture that is at once a historical record, a piece of infrastructure, a landscape, and a remarkable public space. In the Hu Huishan Memorial in Chengdu, he understands that identity is a matter of both collective and personal memory, brilliantly elevating the individual perspective to a foundational element of place-making in order to revive a communal dimension.

Liu Jiakun also seeks a level of technology that is neither high nor low but rather the "appropriate" one based on local wisdom, as well as materials and craftsmanship available. Since his early projects, he has broken the current architectural language to introduce the qualities of simplicity, deriving from the resources at disposal. His sincerity in the use of materials lets them speak for what they are, as their integrity does not require mediation or maintenance. It also enables them to age without fear of deterioration because the collective memory is held within them.

To such available cultural and social resources, Liu Jiakun adds nature, creating new landscapes within the landscape. From the West Village to the Renovation of Tianbao Cave District of Erlang Town in Luzhou, to the Luyeyuan Stone Sculpture Art Museum in Chengdu, the built and natural environments coexist in a reciprocal relation, and in line with the most ancient Chinese philosophy and tradition.

For embracing rather than resisting the dystopia/utopia dualism and showing us how architecture can mediate between reality and idealism; for elevating local solutions into universal visions; and for developing a language that describes a socially and environmentally just world, Liu Jiakun is named the 2025 Pritzker Prize Laureate.

The Department of Sculpture at Sichuan Fine Arts Institute 2004 © Bi Kejian

Shuijingfang Museum, 2013 © Arch-Exist

Hu Huishan Memorial, 2009 © Jiakun Architecture

Luyeyuan Stone Sculpture Art Museum, 2002 © Bi Kejian